American Legal History: A Very Short Introduction

VERY SHORT INTRODUCTIONS are for anyone wanting a stimulating
and accessible way into a new subject. They are written by experts, and
have been translated into more than 45 different languages.

The series began in 1995, and now covers a wide variety of topics in
every discipline. The VSI library now contains over 500 volumes—a Very
Short Introduction to everything from Psychology and Philosophy of
Science to American History and Relativity—and continues to grow in every
subject area.

Titles in the series include the following:

ACCOUNTING Christopher Nobes
ADOLESCENCE Peter K. Smith
ADVERTISING Winston Fletcher
AFRICAN AMERICAN RELIGION
    Eddie S. Glaude Jr
AFRICAN HISTORY John Parker and
    Richard Rathbone
AFRICAN RELIGIONS
    Jacob K. Olupona
AGEING Nancy A. Pachana
AGNOSTICISM Robin Le Poidevin
AGRICULTURE Paul Brassley and
    Richard Soffe
ALEXANDER THE GREAT
    Hugh Bowden
ALGEBRA Peter M. Higgins
AMERICAN HISTORY Paul S. Boyer
AMERICAN IMMIGRATION
    David A. Gerber
AMERICAN LEGAL HISTORY
    G. Edward White
AMERICAN POLITICAL
    HISTORY Donald Critchlow
AMERICAN POLITICAL PARTIES
    AND ELECTIONS L. Sandy Maisel
AMERICAN POLITICS
    Richard M. Valelly
THE AMERICAN
    PRESIDENCY Charles O. Jones
THE AMERICAN REVOLUTION
    Robert J. Allison
AMERICAN SLAVERY
    Heather Andrea Williams
THE AMERICAN WEST Stephen Aron

AMERICAN WOMEN'S HISTORY
    Susan Ware
ANAESTHESIA Aidan O'Donnell
ANARCHISM Colin Ward
ANCIENT ASSYRIA Karen Radner
ANCIENT EGYPT Ian Shaw
ANCIENT EGYPTIAN ART AND
    ARCHITECTURE Christina Riggs
ANCIENT GREECE Paul Cartledge
THE ANCIENT NEAR EAST
    Amanda H. Podany
ANCIENT PHILOSOPHY Julia Annas
ANCIENT WARFARE Harry Sidebottom
ANGELS David Albert Jones
ANGLICANISM Mark Chapman
THE ANGLO-SAXON AGE
    John Blair
ANIMAL BEHAVIOUR
    Tristram D. Wyatt
THE ANIMAL KINGDOM
    Peter Holland
ANIMAL RIGHTS David DeGrazia
THE ANTARCTIC Klaus Dodds
ANTISEMITISM Steven Beller
ANXIETY Daniel Freeman and
    Jason Freeman
THE APOCRYPHAL GOSPELS
    Paul Foster
ARCHAEOLOGY Paul Bahn
ARCHITECTURE Andrew Ballantyne
ARISTOCRACY William Doyle
ARISTOTLE Jonathan Barnes
ART HISTORY Dana Arnold
ART THEORY Cynthia Freeland

ASIAN AMERICAN HISTORY
    Madeline Y. Hsu
ASTROBIOLOGY David C. Catling
ASTROPHYSICS James Binney
ATHEISM Julian Baggini
THE ATMOSPHERE Paul I. Palmer
AUGUSTINE Henry Chadwick
AUSTRALIA Kenneth Morgan
AUTISM Uta Frith
THE AVANT GARDE David Cottington
THE AZTECS David Carrasco
BABYLONIA Trevor Bryce
BACTERIA Sebastian G. B. Amyes
BANKING John Goddard and
    John O. S. Wilson
BARTHES Jonathan Culler
THE BEATS David Sterritt
BEAUTY Roger Scruton
BEHAVIOURAL ECONOMICS
    Michelle Baddeley
BESTSELLERS John Sutherland
THE BIBLE John Riches
BIBLICAL ARCHAEOLOGY Eric H. Cline
BIOGRAPHY Hermione Lee
BLACK HOLES Katherine Blundell
BLOOD Chris Cooper
THE BLUES Elijah Wald
THE BODY Chris Shilling
THE BOOK OF MORMON
    Terryl Givens
BORDERS Alexander C. Diener and
    Joshua Hagen
THE BRAIN Michael O'Shea
THE BRICS Andrew F. Cooper
THE BRITISH CONSTITUTION
    Martin Loughlin
THE BRITISH EMPIRE Ashley Jackson
BRITISH POLITICS Anthony Wright
BUDDHA Michael Carrithers
BUDDHISM Damien Keown
BUDDHIST ETHICS Damien Keown
BYZANTIUM Peter Sarris
CALVINISM Jon Balserak
CANCER Nicholas James
CAPITALISM James Fulcher
CATHOLICISM Gerald O'Collins
CAUSATION Stephen Mumford and
    Rani Lill Anjum
THE CELL Terence Allen and
    Graham Cowling

THE CELTS Barry Cunliffe
CHAOS Leonard Smith
CHEMISTRY Peter Atkins
CHILD PSYCHOLOGY Usha Goswami
CHILDREN'S LITERATURE
    Kimberley Reynolds
CHINESE LITERATURE Sabina Knight
CHOICE THEORY Michael Allingham
CHRISTIAN ART Beth Williamson
CHRISTIAN ETHICS D. Stephen Long
CHRISTIANITY Linda Woodhead
CIRCADIAN RHYTHMS
    Russell Foster and Leon Kreitzman
CITIZENSHIP Richard Bellamy
CIVIL ENGINEERING David Muir Wood
CLASSICAL LITERATURE William Allan
CLASSICAL MYTHOLOGY
    Helen Morales
CLASSICS Mary Beard and John Henderson
CLAUSEWITZ Michael Howard
CLIMATE Mark Maslin
CLIMATE CHANGE Mark Maslin
CLINICAL PSYCHOLOGY Susan
    Llewelyn and Katie Aafjes-van Doorn
COGNITIVE NEUROSCIENCE
    Richard Passingham
THE COLD WAR Robert McMahon
COLONIAL AMERICA Alan Taylor
COLONIAL LATIN AMERICAN
    LITERATURE Rolena Adorno
COMBINATORICS Robin Wilson
COMEDY Matthew Bevis
COMMUNISM Leslie Holmes
COMPLEXITY John H. Holland
THE COMPUTER Darrel Ince
COMPUTER SCIENCE Subrata Dasgupta
CONFUCIANISM Daniel K. Gardner
THE CONQUISTADORS
    Matthew Restall and
    Felipe Fernández-Armesto
CONSCIENCE Paul Strohm
CONSCIOUSNESS Susan Blackmore
CONTEMPORARY ART
    Julian Stallabrass
CONTEMPORARY FICTION
    Robert Eaglestone
CONTINENTAL PHILOSOPHY
    Simon Critchley
COPERNICUS Owen Gingerich
CORAL REEFS Charles Sheppard

CORPORATE SOCIAL
    RESPONSIBILITY Jeremy Moon
CORRUPTION Leslie Holmes
COSMOLOGY Peter Coles
CRIME FICTION Richard Bradford
CRIMINAL JUSTICE Julian V. Roberts
CRITICAL THEORY Stephen Eric Bronner
THE CRUSADES Christopher Tyerman
CRYPTOGRAPHY Fred Piper and
    Sean Murphy
CRYSTALLOGRAPHY A. M. Glazer
THE CULTURAL REVOLUTION
    Richard Curt Kraus
DADA AND SURREALISM
    David Hopkins
DANTE Peter Hainsworth and
    David Robey
DARWIN Jonathan Howard
THE DEAD SEA SCROLLS Timothy Lim
DECOLONIZATION Dane Kennedy
DEMOCRACY Bernard Crick
DEPRESSION Jan Scott and
    Mary Jane Tacchi
DERRIDA Simon Glendinning
DESCARTES Tom Sorell
DESERTS Nick Middleton
DESIGN John Heskett
DEVELOPMENTAL BIOLOGY
    Lewis Wolpert
THE DEVIL Darren Oldridge
DIASPORA Kevin Kenny
DICTIONARIES Lynda Mugglestone
DINOSAURS David Norman
DIPLOMACY Joseph M. Siracusa
DOCUMENTARY FILM
    Patricia Aufderheide
DREAMING J. Allan Hobson
DRUGS Les Iversen
DRUIDS Barry Cunliffe
EARLY MUSIC Thomas Forrest Kelly
THE EARTH Martin Redfern
EARTH SYSTEM SCIENCE Tim Lenton
ECONOMICS Partha Dasgupta
EDUCATION Gary Thomas
EGYPTIAN MYTH Geraldine Pinch
EIGHTEENTH-CENTURY BRITAIN
    Paul Langford
THE ELEMENTS Philip Ball
EMOTION Dylan Evans
EMPIRE Stephen Howe

ENGELS Terrell Carver
ENGINEERING David Blockley
ENGLISH LITERATURE Jonathan Bate
THE ENLIGHTENMENT
    John Robertson
ENTREPRENEURSHIP Paul Westhead
    and Mike Wright
ENVIRONMENTAL ECONOMICS
    Stephen Smith
ENVIRONMENTAL POLITICS
    Andrew Dobson
EPICUREANISM Catherine Wilson
EPIDEMIOLOGY Rodolfo Saracci
ETHICS Simon Blackburn
ETHNOMUSICOLOGY Timothy Rice
THE ETRUSCANS Christopher Smith
EUGENICS Philippa Levine
THE EUROPEAN UNION John Pinder
    and Simon Usherwood
EVOLUTION Brian and
    Deborah Charlesworth
EXISTENTIALISM Thomas Flynn
EXPLORATION Stewart A. Weaver
THE EYE Michael Land
FAMILY LAW Jonathan Herring
FASCISM Kevin Passmore
FASHION Rebecca Arnold
FEMINISM Margaret Walters
FILM Michael Wood
FILM MUSIC Kathryn Kalinak
THE FIRST WORLD WAR
    Michael Howard
FOLK MUSIC Mark Slobin
FOOD John Krebs
FORENSIC PSYCHOLOGY
    David Canter
FORENSIC SCIENCE Jim Fraser
FORESTS Jaboury Ghazoul
FOSSILS Keith Thomson
FOUCAULT Gary Gutting
THE FOUNDING FATHERS
    R. B. Bernstein
FRACTALS Kenneth Falconer
FREE SPEECH Nigel Warburton
FREE WILL Thomas Pink
FRENCH LITERATURE John D. Lyons
THE FRENCH REVOLUTION
    William Doyle
FREUD Anthony Storr
FUNDAMENTALISM Malise Ruthven

FUNGI Nicholas P. Money
THE FUTURE Jennifer M. Gidley
GALAXIES John Gribbin
GALILEO Stillman Drake
GAME THEORY Ken Binmore
GANDHI Bhikhu Parekh
GENES Jonathan Slack
GENIUS Andrew Robinson
GEOGRAPHY John Matthews and
    David Herbert
GEOPOLITICS Klaus Dodds
GERMAN LITERATURE Nicholas Boyle
GERMAN PHILOSOPHY Andrew Bowie
GLOBAL CATASTROPHES Bill McGuire
GLOBAL ECONOMIC HISTORY
    Robert C. Allen
GLOBALIZATION Manfred Steger
GOD John Bowker
GOETHE Ritchie Robertson
THE GOTHIC Nick Groom
GOVERNANCE Mark Bevir
GRAVITY Timothy Clifton
THE GREAT DEPRESSION AND THE
    NEW DEAL Eric Rauchway
HABERMAS James Gordon Finlayson
THE HABSBURG EMPIRE
    Martyn Rady
HAPPINESS Daniel M. Haybron
THE HARLEM RENAISSANCE
    Cheryl A. Wall
THE HEBREW BIBLE AS LITERATURE
    Tod Linafelt
HEGEL Peter Singer
HEIDEGGER Michael Inwood
HERMENEUTICS Jens Zimmermann
HERODOTUS Jennifer T. Roberts
HIEROGLYPHS Penelope Wilson
HINDUISM Kim Knott
HISTORY John H. Arnold
THE HISTORY OF ASTRONOMY
    Michael Hoskin
THE HISTORY OF CHEMISTRY
    William H. Brock
THE HISTORY OF LIFE Michael Benton
THE HISTORY OF MATHEMATICS
    Jacqueline Stedall
THE HISTORY OF MEDICINE
    William Bynum
THE HISTORY OF TIME Leofranc
    Holford-Strevens

HIV AND AIDS Alan Whiteside
HOBBES Richard Tuck
HOLLYWOOD Peter Decherney
HOME Michael Allen Fox
HORMONES Martin Luck
HUMAN ANATOMY Leslie Klenerman
HUMAN EVOLUTION Bernard Wood
HUMAN RIGHTS Andrew Clapham
HUMANISM Stephen Law
HUME A. J. Ayer
HUMOUR Noël Carroll
THE ICE AGE Jamie Woodward
IDEOLOGY Michael Freeden
INDIAN CINEMA Ashish Rajadhyaksha
INDIAN PHILOSOPHY Sue Hamilton
THE INDUSTRIAL REVOLUTION
    Robert C. Allen
INFECTIOUS DISEASE Marta L. Wayne
    and Benjamin M. Bolker
INFINITY Ian Stewart
INFORMATION Luciano Floridi
INNOVATION Mark Dodgson and
    David Gann
INTELLIGENCE Ian J. Deary
INTELLECTUAL PROPERTY
    Siva Vaidhyanathan
INTERNATIONAL LAW
    Vaughan Lowe
INTERNATIONAL
    MIGRATION Khalid Koser
INTERNATIONAL RELATIONS
    Paul Wilkinson
INTERNATIONAL SECURITY
    Christopher S. Browning
IRAN Ali M. Ansari
ISLAM Malise Ruthven
ISLAMIC HISTORY Adam Silverstein
ISOTOPES Rob Ellam
ITALIAN LITERATURE
    Peter Hainsworth and David Robey
JESUS Richard Bauckham
JOURNALISM Ian Hargreaves
JUDAISM Norman Solomon
JUNG Anthony Stevens
KABBALAH Joseph Dan
KAFKA Ritchie Robertson
KANT Roger Scruton
KEYNES Robert Skidelsky
KIERKEGAARD Patrick Gardiner
KNOWLEDGE Jennifer Nagel

THE KORAN Michael Cook
LANDSCAPE ARCHITECTURE
    Ian H. Thompson
LANDSCAPES AND
    GEOMORPHOLOGY
    Andrew Goudie and Heather Viles
LANGUAGES Stephen R. Anderson
LATE ANTIQUITY Gillian Clark
LAW Raymond Wacks
THE LAWS OF THERMODYNAMICS
    Peter Atkins
LEADERSHIP Keith Grint
LEARNING Mark Haselgrove
LEIBNIZ Maria Rosa Antognazza
LIBERALISM Michael Freeden
LIGHT Ian Walmsley
LINCOLN Allen C. Guelzo
LINGUISTICS Peter Matthews
LITERARY THEORY Jonathan Culler
LOCKE John Dunn
LOGIC Graham Priest
LOVE Ronald de Sousa
MACHIAVELLI Quentin Skinner
MADNESS Andrew Scull
MAGIC Owen Davies
MAGNA CARTA Nicholas Vincent
MAGNETISM Stephen Blundell
MALTHUS Donald Winch
MANAGEMENT John Hendry
MAO Delia Davin
MARINE BIOLOGY Philip V. Mladenov
THE MARQUIS DE SADE John Phillips
MARTIN LUTHER Scott H. Hendrix
MARTYRDOM Jolyon Mitchell
MARX Peter Singer
MATERIALS Christopher Hall
MATHEMATICS Timothy Gowers
THE MEANING OF LIFE
    Terry Eagleton
MEASUREMENT David Hand
MEDICAL ETHICS Tony Hope
MEDICAL LAW Charles Foster
MEDIEVAL BRITAIN John Gillingham
    and Ralph A. Griffiths
MEDIEVAL LITERATURE
    Elaine Treharne
MEDIEVAL PHILOSOPHY
    John Marenbon
MEMORY Jonathan K. Foster
METAPHYSICS Stephen Mumford

THE MEXICAN REVOLUTION
    Alan Knight
MICHAEL FARADAY Frank A. J. L. James
MICROBIOLOGY Nicholas P. Money
MICROECONOMICS Avinash Dixit
MICROSCOPY Terence Allen
THE MIDDLE AGES Miri Rubin
MILITARY JUSTICE Eugene R. Fidell
MINERALS David Vaughan
MODERN ART David Cottington
MODERN CHINA Rana Mitter
MODERN DRAMA
    Kirsten E. Shepherd-Barr
MODERN FRANCE Vanessa R. Schwartz
MODERN IRELAND Senia Pašeta
MODERN ITALY Anna Cento Bull
MODERN JAPAN
    Christopher Goto-Jones
MODERN LATIN AMERICAN
    LITERATURE
    Roberto González Echevarría
MODERN WAR Richard English
MODERNISM Christopher Butler
MOLECULAR BIOLOGY Aysha Divan
    and Janice A. Royds
MOLECULES Philip Ball
THE MONGOLS Morris Rossabi
MOONS David A. Rothery
MORMONISM
    Richard Lyman Bushman
MOUNTAINS Martin F. Price
MUHAMMAD Jonathan A. C. Brown
MULTICULTURALISM Ali Rattansi
MUSIC Nicholas Cook
MYTH Robert A. Segal
THE NAPOLEONIC WARS
    Mike Rapport
NATIONALISM Steven Grosby
NAVIGATION Jim Bennett
NELSON MANDELA Elleke Boehmer
NEOLIBERALISM Manfred Steger and
    Ravi Roy
NETWORKS Guido Caldarelli and
    Michele Catanzaro
THE NEW TESTAMENT
    Luke Timothy Johnson
THE NEW TESTAMENT AS
    LITERATURE Kyle Keefer
NEWTON Robert Iliffe
NIETZSCHE Michael Tanner

NINETEENTH-CENTURY BRITAIN
    Christopher Harvie and
    H. C. G. Matthew
THE NORMAN CONQUEST
    George Garnett
NORTH AMERICAN INDIANS
    Theda Perdue and Michael D. Green
NORTHERN IRELAND
    Marc Mulholland
NOTHING Frank Close
NUCLEAR PHYSICS Frank Close
NUCLEAR POWER Maxwell Irvine
NUCLEAR WEAPONS
    Joseph M. Siracusa
NUMBERS Peter M. Higgins
NUTRITION David A. Bender
OBJECTIVITY Stephen Gaukroger
THE OLD TESTAMENT
    Michael D. Coogan
THE ORCHESTRA D. Kern Holoman
ORGANIC CHEMISTRY
    Graham Patrick
ORGANIZATIONS Mary Jo Hatch
PAGANISM Owen Davies
THE PALESTINIAN-ISRAELI
    CONFLICT Martin Bunton
PANDEMICS Christian W. McMillen
PARTICLE PHYSICS Frank Close
PAUL E. P. Sanders
PEACE Oliver P. Richmond
PENTECOSTALISM William K. Kay
THE PERIODIC TABLE Eric R. Scerri
PHILOSOPHY Edward Craig
PHILOSOPHY IN THE ISLAMIC
    WORLD Peter Adamson
PHILOSOPHY OF LAW
    Raymond Wacks
PHILOSOPHY OF SCIENCE
    Samir Okasha
PHOTOGRAPHY Steve Edwards
PHYSICAL CHEMISTRY Peter Atkins
PILGRIMAGE Ian Reader
PLAGUE Paul Slack
PLANETS David A. Rothery
PLANTS Timothy Walker
PLATE TECTONICS Peter Molnar
PLATO Julia Annas
POLITICAL PHILOSOPHY
    David Miller
POLITICS Kenneth Minogue

POPULISM Cas Mudde and
    Cristóbal Rovira Kaltwasser
POSTCOLONIALISM Robert Young
POSTMODERNISM Christopher Butler
POSTSTRUCTURALISM
    Catherine Belsey
PREHISTORY Chris Gosden
PRESOCRATIC PHILOSOPHY
    Catherine Osborne
PRIVACY Raymond Wacks
PROBABILITY John Haigh
PROGRESSIVISM Walter Nugent
PROTESTANTISM Mark A. Noll
PSYCHIATRY Tom Burns
PSYCHOANALYSIS Daniel Pick
PSYCHOLOGY Gillian Butler and
    Freda McManus
PSYCHOTHERAPY Tom Burns and
    Eva Burns-Lundgren
PUBLIC ADMINISTRATION
    Stella Z. Theodoulou and Ravi K. Roy
PUBLIC HEALTH Virginia Berridge
PURITANISM Francis J. Bremer
THE QUAKERS Pink Dandelion
QUANTUM THEORY
    John Polkinghorne
RACISM Ali Rattansi
RADIOACTIVITY Claudio Tuniz
RASTAFARI Ennis B. Edmonds
THE REAGAN REVOLUTION Gil Troy
REALITY Jan Westerhoff
THE REFORMATION Peter Marshall
RELATIVITY Russell Stannard
RELIGION IN AMERICA Timothy Beal
THE RENAISSANCE Jerry Brotton
RENAISSANCE ART
    Geraldine A. Johnson
REVOLUTIONS Jack A. Goldstone
RHETORIC Richard Toye
RISK Baruch Fischhoff and John Kadvany
RITUAL Barry Stephenson
RIVERS Nick Middleton
ROBOTICS Alan Winfield
ROCKS Jan Zalasiewicz
ROMAN BRITAIN Peter Salway
THE ROMAN EMPIRE
    Christopher Kelly
THE ROMAN REPUBLIC
    David M. Gwynn
ROMANTICISM Michael Ferber

ROUSSEAU Robert Wokler
RUSSELL A. C. Grayling
RUSSIAN HISTORY Geoffrey Hosking
RUSSIAN LITERATURE Catriona Kelly
THE RUSSIAN REVOLUTION
  S. A. Smith
SAVANNAS Peter A. Furley
SCHIZOPHRENIA Chris Frith and
  Eve Johnstone
SCHOPENHAUER Christopher Janaway
SCIENCE AND RELIGION
  Thomas Dixon
SCIENCE FICTION David Seed
THE SCIENTIFIC REVOLUTION
  Lawrence M. Principe
SCOTLAND Rab Houston
SEXUALITY Véronique Mottier
SHAKESPEARE'S COMEDIES
  Bart van Es
SIKHISM Eleanor Nesbitt
THE SILK ROAD James A. Millward
SLANG Jonathon Green
SLEEP Steven W. Lockley and
  Russell G. Foster
SOCIAL AND CULTURAL
  ANTHROPOLOGY
  John Monaghan and Peter Just
SOCIAL PSYCHOLOGY Richard J. Crisp
SOCIAL WORK Sally Holland and
  Jonathan Scourfield
SOCIALISM Michael Newman
SOCIOLINGUISTICS John Edwards
SOCIOLOGY Steve Bruce
SOCRATES C. C. W. Taylor
SOUND Mike Goldsmith
THE SOVIET UNION Stephen Lovell
THE SPANISH CIVIL WAR
  Helen Graham
SPANISH LITERATURE Jo Labanyi
SPINOZA Roger Scruton
SPIRITUALITY Philip Sheldrake
SPORT Mike Cronin
STARS Andrew King
STATISTICS David J. Hand
STEM CELLS Jonathan Slack
STRUCTURAL ENGINEERING
  David Blockley
STUART BRITAIN John Morrill

SUPERCONDUCTIVITY
  Stephen Blundell
SYMMETRY Ian Stewart
TAXATION Stephen Smith
TEETH Peter S. Ungar
TELESCOPES Geoff Cottrell
TERRORISM Charles Townshend
THEATRE Marvin Carlson
THEOLOGY David F. Ford
THOMAS AQUINAS Fergus Kerr
THOUGHT Tim Bayne
TIBETAN BUDDHISM
  Matthew T. Kapstein
TOCQUEVILLE Harvey C. Mansfield
TRAGEDY Adrian Poole
TRANSLATION Matthew Reynolds
THE TROJAN WAR Eric H. Cline
TRUST Katherine Hawley
THE TUDORS John Guy
TWENTIETH-CENTURY BRITAIN
  Kenneth O. Morgan
THE UNITED NATIONS
  Jussi M. Hanhimäki
THE U.S. CONGRESS Donald A. Ritchie
THE U.S. SUPREME COURT
  Linda Greenhouse
UTOPIANISM Lyman Tower Sargent
THE VIKINGS Julian Richards
VIRUSES Dorothy H. Crawford
VOLTAIRE Nicholas Cronk
WAR AND TECHNOLOGY
  Alex Roland
WATER John Finney
WEATHER Storm Dunlop
THE WELFARE STATE
  David Garland
WILLIAM SHAKESPEARE
  Stanley Wells
WITCHCRAFT Malcolm Gaskill
WITTGENSTEIN A. C. Grayling
WORK Stephen Fineman
WORLD MUSIC Philip Bohlman
THE WORLD TRADE
  ORGANIZATION Amrita Narlikar
WORLD WAR II Gerhard L. Weinberg
WRITING AND SCRIPT
  Andrew Robinson
ZIONISM Michael Stanislawski

G. Edward White

AMERICAN LEGAL HISTORY

A Very Short Introduction

OXFORD
UNIVERSITY PRESS

Oxford University Press is a department of the University of Oxford.
It furthers the University's objective of excellence in research,
scholarship, and education by publishing worldwide.

Oxford   New York
Auckland   Cape Town   Dar es Salaam   Hong Kong   Karachi
Kuala Lumpur   Madrid   Melbourne   Mexico City   Nairobi
New Delhi   Shanghai   Taipei   Toronto

With offices in
Argentina   Austria   Brazil   Chile   Czech Republic   France   Greece
Guatemala   Hungary   Italy   Japan   Poland   Portugal   Singapore
South Korea   Switzerland   Thailand   Turkey   Ukraine   Vietnam

Oxford is a registered trademark of Oxford University Press
in the UK and certain other countries.

Published in the United States of America by
Oxford University Press
198 Madison Avenue, New York, NY 10016

© Oxford University Press 2014

Library of Congress Cataloging-in-Publication Data
White, G. Edward.
American legal history : a very short introduction / G. Edward White.
pages   cm
Includes bibliographical references and index.
ISBN 978-0-19-976600-0 (pbk.)
1. Law—United States—History. I. Title.
KF352.W485   2013
349.73—dc23   2013021284

5 7 9 8 6 4

Printed in Great Britain
by Ashford Colour Press Ltd., Gosport, Hants.
on acid-free paper

For Susan Davis White

Contents

List of illustrations xv

Acknowledgments xvii

Introduction 1

1 The legal history of Indian tribes 3

2 Law and African American slavery 17

3 Rights of property and their regulation 32

4 Law and entrepreneurship 45

5 Criminal law 68

6 Law and domestic relations 82

7 Civil injuries and the law of torts 96

8 Legal education and the legal profession 112

Epilogue 127

References 131

Further reading 135

Index 139

List of illustrations

1 Lakota (Sioux) chiefs
  ceremony, 1891 **6**
  Library of Congress LC-DIG-
  ppmsc-02513

2 Slave auction in the South
  from *Harper's Weekly*, July 13,
  1861. Sketch by Theodore
  R. Davis **21**
  Library of Congress LC-USZ62-2582

3 Sheriff's sale of real estate,
  Bucks County, Pennsylvania,
  February 4, 1880 **37**
  Library of Congress LC-USZC2-153

4 Emigrant party crossing
  the Rocky Mountains to
  California, 1850 **50**
  Library of Congress LC-DIG-
  ppmsca-02887

5 Woman listening to radio **62**
  Photograph by Underwood &
  Underwood. Library of Congress
  LC-USZ62-23645

6 Overcrowding in a California
  prison, photograph appended
  to the Supreme Court's
  opinion in *Brown v. Plata*, 131
  S.Ct. 1910 (2011) **80**
  California Department of Corrections

7 Applicants for marriage
  licenses at New York City
  marriage bureau,
  mid-1920s **93**
  Photograph by George Grantham
  Bain. Bain Collection, Library of
  Congress LC-DIGggbain-24188

8 Wreck on Long Island Railroad,
  Fifth Avenue, Bayshore,
  New York, July 10, 1909 **103**
  Photograph by M. J. Anderson.
  Library of Congress LC-USZ62-25401

9 The Posey Building,
  Shawneetown, Illinois, where
  Abraham Lincoln had a law
  office **120**
  Photograph by Russell Lee, 1937.
  Library of Congress LC-USF341-T01-
  010685-B

10 John Jeffries teaches class at
   University of Virginia School
   of Law **124**
   Photo by Ian Bradshaw, courtesy
   University of Virginia School of Law.

Acknowledgments

Once again the reference librarians at the University of Virginia School of Law have given me invaluable assistance in the preparation of this book. In this instance, Kristin Glover deserves special recognition for her work in securing illustrations that were relevant to the book's coverage but did not, in most cases, present complicated permissions problems. Thanks also to Mary Wood, the School of Law's director of communications, for her help with procuring some of the illustrations. James Barolo of the Virginia School of Law class of 2014 read an earlier draft of the manuscript and gave me helpful critical suggestions. Nancy Toff of Oxford University Press encouraged me, in her usual lively manner, to undertake this book and kept on me until I completed it.

Acknowledgments

I owe to the reference librarians at the University of Virginia School of Law have given me invaluable assistance. In the preparation of this book, in this instance, Kristin Glover deserves special recognition for her work in securing illustrations that were relevant to the book's coverage but did not, in most cases, pre-exist consolidated in a single archive or file. Thanks also to Mary Wood, the Law School's director of communications, for her help with procuring some of the illustrations. Lana of the Virginia School of Law who helped in earlier drafts of the manuscript and to Emma Perez-Trevino... has... in her usual lively manner to... who stuck on the task and kept on me until I completed it.

Introduction

Law has played a central role in American history. Legal ideas and issues were paramount in the decision of the colonies in North America to secede from the British empire. Law facilitated the marginalization of American Indian tribes and the accompanying expansion of territory and settlement that marked the emergence of the United States as a major power in the nineteenth century. The inability of the existing branches of government, and of the major political parties, to find an enduring legal solution to the problem of African American slavery helped precipitate the Civil War. The Supreme Court and its interpretations of the U.S. Constitution, in cases affecting interstate commerce, international treaties, civil rights, race relations, and intimate same-sex relationships, have directly affected the lives of countless American citizens. To review the course of American legal history is to confront defining issues in the development of American civilization.

In addition, law permeates every facet of American life. The governmental institutions of the United States are undergirded by law. Law regulates our elected and appointed officials, from the president of the United States to police assigned to traffic duties. Law determines the qualifications for American citizenship and who is eligible to enter the United States. The basic transactions that compose people's lives, such as marriage, divorce, home and car ownership, and entering and leaving the public schools, are regulated by law.

Moreover, law is an aspirational force in American society. We are said to live under a "rule of law," which means that Americans expect the settlement of disputes to be peacefully resolved through the processes of legal institutions, rather than being resolved by power or force. Americans also expect individual citizens to be treated equally, and fairly, by the legal system, although historically that was often not the case, and few would claim that current legal institutions have done a perfect job in redressing inequalities and injustices. Nonetheless, most Americans believe that they have the "right" to appeal to the legal system to respond to personal grievances and that the system is designed to insure fairness and justice for ordinary citizens.

Because law is so pervasive a dimension of American life, its history is particularly important. In that history, one becomes introduced to the central defining themes of American culture: geographic isolation, economic abundance, transatlantic settlement, the relations between European settlers and indigenous tribes, African American slavery, the importance of agricultural householding, the growth of industrial enterprise and urbanization, the emergence of the United States as a world power. In reviewing that history, one becomes aware that law has been intimately connected to each of those themes, reacting to them and helping to shape them. To study American legal history is to come in contact with the forces that have given the United States its unique identity.

The subject of American legal history is sufficiently diverse and vast as to preclude including all of its topics in this book. I have therefore limited myself primarily to domestic legal issues and private law themes. I have emphasized common law judicial decisions and legislation more than constitutional developments. And I have sought to focus on topics and issues that are connected to central themes in American history.

Chapter 1
The legal history of
Indian tribes

The most fundamental theme of American legal history in the
sixteenth and seventeenth centuries was the interaction of
European settlers with the aboriginal tribes who inhabited the
North American continent. The settlers mistakenly gave them the
name "Indians" because when Christopher Columbus had reached
the Bahamian island he named San Salvador in 1492, he believed
he had reached "the Indies," the name given to India and China
by previous European explorers. Columbus called the indigenous
tribes of San Salvador "los Indios," and later settlers perpetuated
the name.

The first step in the successful creation of European settlements
in North America was an accommodation with the tribes, who
vastly outnumbered European settlers in America through the
eighteenth century and remained the primary inhabitants of the
western portions of the continent through the end of the Civil War.

Law played a central role in that accommodation, and its terms
were far more favorable to the European settlers and their
descendants than to the tribes. Alexis de Tocqueville, in his early
nineteenth-century book *Democracy in America*, maintained that
British and American settlers—in contrast to the Spanish, who
from the 1500s on had subdued aboriginal tribes in Central and
South America with military force—had interacted with North

American tribes "quietly, legally, and philanthropically, without spilling blood . . . in a regular, and, so to say, quite legal manner."

Tocqueville's comment captured the fact that when tribes posed some kind of threat to European settlements in America, settlers did not typically seek to overcome them militarily. Instead they turned to law, by which they deprived them of their land, forced them to relocate to areas remote from settlements, and eventually placed them on reservations, where they were treated as wards of the federal government. The history of the legal treatment of American Indian tribes can be divided into distinct phases of settler-tribal accommodation. In all but the last phase, the interaction between tribes and settlers disadvantaged the tribes.

The contact phase

The ancestors of the North American tribes whom the first European settlers encountered had originally arrived by traveling long distances over land bridges from Asia and for centuries had found North America an environment easily capable of supporting agricultural and hunter-gatherer societies. Tribes lived off the land, typically moving from place to place in search of food or places to plant crops. Their environmental practices included symbiotic crop growing and the controlled burning of forests to facilitate the regeneration of nutriments in the soil. They organized themselves in clans and extended families, emphasizing intermarriage and collective uses of property. Aboriginal tribes did not enclose land, and most of their settlements were mobile, driven by seasonal changes. Individual tribes tended to return to the same areas at given times of the year and to treat those areas as "reserved" for them, and in some instances had hostile relations with other tribes who occupied adjacent areas.

Members of clans were ranked hierarchically, with one member of a clan serving as sachem, or head of a set of clans. When a member of a clan injured or killed a member of another clan, reciprocal payment was expected, sometimes in the form of a human sacrifice and other times in some other form of compensation. Males and females engaged in different work activities: men served as hunters and gatherers and women as agricultural workers and child-rearers. When seasonal climates precluded hunting or gathering, men engaged in leisure pursuits, such as athletics or gambling; women's leisure opportunities were limited.

Social interactions within and between the tribes took common forms. None of the tribes on the American continent had a written language. Important group events involved extensive oral ceremonies, including lengthy speeches, the smoking of pipes, and the exchange of gifts. Because tribes often had their own distinct languages, interpreters—people who had come into extensive contacts with other tribes—were common in most tribal negotiations. Grievances and other policy decisions were resolved collectively, with participants' social positions sometimes affecting the weight afforded to their remarks. All tribes practiced some form of spiritual worship, which tended to emphasize relationships among humans and beings of the natural world, such as animals, trees, stars, and bodies of water.

These defining characteristics of tribal life were utterly unfamiliar to sixteenth- and seventeenth-century European voyagers to the North American continent. Most of them practiced a form of Christianity and accepted that religion's explanations of events in the universe. By the seventeenth century, European communities had come to emphasize the clearing and cultivating of land, and the use of domestic animals in that process, as part of establishing settlements. The tribes, in contrast, did not keep domestic animals, did not enclose the areas they occupied, often did not remain in any particular place for an extended period of time, and were unable to read or write languages. In many respects, tribal members seemed, to the settlers who encountered them, "primitive," "pagan," or "savage" beings.

1. The delegation of chiefs from the Lakota tribe who settled the "Indian war" in Dakota Territory in 1891. Photograph probably taken on or near the Pine Ridge Indian Reservation.

Soon after the first contacts between tribes and European settlers, diseases began to spread among tribes, and conflicts surfaced over the uses of land. Settlers brought domestic animals carrying bacterial microbes to North America that invaded tribal populations and created "virgin soil" epidemics (caused by bacteria to which the infected population had built up no immunities). The epidemics significantly reduced tribal populations in the early seventeenth century. Meanwhile, settlers began to enclose land, disrupting tribal practices that emphasized the use rather than the exclusive possession of areas suitable for hunting or agriculture.

As these disruptions developed into conflicts, the settlers began to turn to European (mainly English) law in order to address the customs and practices of tribes. When territorial disputes between tribes and settlers surfaced, both groups had difficulty determining two basic legal issues: jurisdiction—the power to entertain and resolve legal disputes, and liability—the grounds for redressing damage.

European settlements established colonial courts early on in their formation. The question whether tribal members ought to be subject to the jurisdiction of those courts became a major source of controversy between tribes and settlers. They typically came to understandings that colonial courts had the power to resolve disputes arising from minor injuries to persons and damage to personal property, but more serious injuries and land disputes posed difficulties. When tribal members killed or injured other tribal members and were made subject to the jurisdiction of settler courts, tribes were offended. "King Philip's war," an uprising of tribes against settlements in Massachusetts in 1675, was a reaction to the settlers having tried and hanged three members of the Wampanoag tribe for murdering an Indian living in a colonial settlement. Meanwhile, disputes over land use became endemic.

Over the eighteenth and nineteenth centuries, the social and legal relationships forged in the initial contact phase of European settlement on the North American continent served as a framework for the ongoing interaction of Amerindian tribes and American settlers of European descent. As that framework persisted, it underwent significant modifications.

Over time, tribes living near settlements increasingly found their members subject to the jurisdiction of colonial courts. This forced tribes either to attach themselves to colonial settlements or to withdraw into "unsettled" areas of the North American continent. By the mid-eighteenth century, almost all of the tribes originally inhabiting the Atlantic coast had withdrawn into the continent's interior. Meanwhile, the English population of colonial America had grown rapidly, and settlers had steadily moved westward. For the next 150-odd years, these trends would continue, as the legal history of Amerindians took on progressively darker casts.

Postcontact phases

"Next to the case of the black race within our bosom," James Madison wrote to James Monroe in 1824, "that of the red on our borders is the problem most baffling to the policy of the country." As the United States of America expanded its territory, prospered, fought a civil war, and emerged as a world geopolitical force in the nineteenth and early twentieth centuries, the problem of "the red man" inhabiting the "borders" of westward settlement by Americans of European stock remained as "baffling" a policy issue as that of African American slavery.

From the founding of the United States of America in the late eighteenth century through the 1930s, the framework of settler-tribal interactions established in the contact phase remained largely intact. But the legal relationships between settlers and tribes were successively modified as the territory of the United States dramatically expanded, settlers moved relentlessly westward, and state governments and the federal government expanded their presence. Almost all of the modifications were disadvantageous to tribes.

The modifications took three different forms, each of which reflected stages in the legal and social history of Amerindian tribes after they first made contact with European voyagers.

Initial stage (1754–1783)

Wars involving European powers and the British colonists in America swept through the eastern portions of North America between 1754 and 1783, and tribes could not avoid becoming involved. On the whole, they tended to form allegiances with the losing sides: with the French against the English in the Seven Years War and with Great Britain in the American Revolution. In 1763 the British government—after driving the French, who had made partnerships with tribes in commercial hunting, fishing, and trading ventures, out of what became the United States—established a western boundary "line" designed to prevent settlers from encroaching on territory reserved for tribes. American settlers ignored this line, cleared forests, claimed and enclosed land, and sought the help of local and state governments in their efforts. By the time of Madison's comments to Monroe, these encroachments had displaced tribes from their traditional hunting and agricultural grounds along the western portions of the original seaboard colonies, stretching from what became Maine to Georgia.

Second stage (1783–1860)

At the time Madison wrote Monroe about the "red [race] on our borders," the federal government had become the sole entity empowered to enter into agreements with tribes and establish policies affecting them. Some states, however, claimed the power to control the conduct of tribes located within their borders. The vast amount of territory acquired by the United States in the 1803 Louisiana Purchase and an 1819 treaty with Spain was primarily occupied by tribes, making the issue of who "owned" those lands more critical. Coastal states began selling what they called "preemptive" rights to unsettled lands within their borders, meaning that a settler buying land from the state had superior title to any other claimant. The basis for the title came from the state's claim that it owned the land, either because of a colonial grant, discovery, or the conquest of a tribe.

This practice raised the question of the legitimacy of what was termed an "Indian title," one derived from a transfer of land "owned" by tribes to settlers. The legitimacy of "Indian titles" to land was considered by the Supreme Court in *Johnson v. McIntosh* (1823). Chief Justice John Marshall declared, on behalf of all his fellow justices, that when European nations had settled America they had obtained "fee simple" ownership of Indian lands (uncontested title to those lands) through discovery or conquest, so "Indian titles" amounted only to rights of occupancy. The decision assured that states did not have to formally purchase tribal lands before selling them to settlers.

Johnson v. McIntosh was the first of three Marshall Court decisions in the 1820s and 1830s that marginalized the legal status of Amerindian tribes. Part of Marshall's rationale for characterizing Indian titles to land as granting only occupancy rights was that Indians were "fierce savages" who stood in the way of settlement. However, as "savages" tribes presented a problem of governance as the American nation expanded westward into "Indian territory." That problem was solved by making tribes wards of the federal government and removing them from states where their presence formed a barrier to settlement. Two Marshall Court decisions, *Cherokee Nation v. Georgia* and *Worcester v. Georgia*, justified these policies.

Despite the fact that the Cherokee tribe had long been established within Georgia's boundaries, that state's legislature passed a series of laws abolishing Cherokee government and distributing Cherokee lands to white settlers. The Cherokees challenged the constitutionality of these laws, maintaining that treaties they had entered into with the federal government in which their rights to lands they occupied had been recognized should prevent Georgia from acting. They also claimed that article III of the Constitution, which gave the Supreme Court jurisdiction over cases involving "foreign states," required the Court to hear their appeal, because the Cherokee nation, as evidenced by its treaties with the United States, was a foreign state.

Cherokee Nation and the subsequent *Worcester* case, in which two non-Cherokee ministers were imprisoned under one of the Georgia laws for preaching within the Cherokee nation, posed difficulties for the Marshall Court. The Court's narrow holding in *Cherokee Nation* was that it lacked jurisdiction to hear disputes between states and Indian tribes. Along the way, however, a minority of justices concluded that the Cherokee nation was a "domestic dependent nation": it had territorial integrity and powers of self-government but was in a relationship with the federal government that "resembled that of a ward to its guardian." The minority's conclusion, articulated in an opinion by Marshall, announced that the federal government held a "trust" relationship with tribes, even though there was no constitutional basis for that claim.

Marshall's opinion in *Cherokee Nation* also intimated that the states had no power to regulate the affairs of Indian tribes within their borders or to enter into treaties or other legal agreements with them. That intimation was openly endorsed by the Court in *Worcester:* Marshall, for the Court, found that the sole governmental body authorized to regulate affairs with tribes was the federal government.

Although *Cherokee Nation* and *Worcester* cemented the propositions that the federal government was the exclusive agent for dealing with tribes and that tribes were its wards, those conclusions were not based on the Constitution. Rather, they were based on the experience of settler-tribal interactions over two centuries of American history, which had resulted in tribal members losing their land, being reduced to marginal status in settler communities, and progressively retreating or being forcibly relocated to regions west of the line of frontier settlement. In the years after *Worcester*, the federal government took for granted that it was the exclusive agent for engaging in intercourse with tribes and managing tribal affairs.

Third stage (1860s to 1940s)

After *Worcester*, it was clear that states could not force tribes to give up their lands or force them out of state territory. Nonetheless, the federal government, mindful of the constant pressure from settlers to acquire tribal lands, confronted tribes with the threat of eventually losing their lands if they did not agree to relocate to western regions. The result was a series of treaties between the United States and tribes in which the tribes, in exchange for relinquishing land in states east of the Mississippi, were given large tracts of land in federal territories in the trans-Mississippi west. By the 1840s, "removal," as it was called, had resulted in tribes possessing large areas of land stretching from Minnesota to Texas.

Removal, however, proved only a temporary solution to the problem of tribes standing in the way of continued white settlement of the West. By the 1850s, after gold was discovered in California, settlers seeking routes to the West Coast poured into the trans-Mississippi west, and the railroad industry began to establish lines west of the Mississippi. The Bureau of Indian Affairs lacked the resources to prevent conflicts between settlers and tribes along emigration routes, and the idea of preventing settler emigration was never contemplated. Further relocation of tribes appeared to be the only solution.

The idea of Indian reservations emerged out of settler demand for access to emigration routes in the trans-Mississippi west. Between the 1850s and 1880s, the federal government entered into agreements with tribes in which the tribes ceded large portions of land that had been allocated to them in previous treaties. In exchange the tribes "reserved" other portions of land, with distinct boundaries, for their own use. Those "reservations" of tribal land were designed to create autonomous regions where tribes would govern themselves, undisturbed by settlers.

Although the idea of reservations originally had some humanitarian dimensions—proponents of the reservation model maintained that it would preserve tribal autonomy and afford the tribes secure possession of their land—the main purpose of reservations was to keep tribes out of the way of expanding settlement. By the 1880s, nearly all of the public land in the area between the Mississippi River and the Pacific coast had been acquired by the federal government and was dotted with reservations.

The reservation system accomplished its purpose, clearing the way for white settlement of the trans-Mississippi west. But it encountered difficulties after the Civil War. The original humanitarian conception of Indian reservations allowed tribes space where they could retain their traditional ways of life without contact with settlers that disadvantaged them. But problems arose in maintaining that space. Boundaries were drawn every time a new reservation was created, but additional white settlement in areas adjacent to reservations put pressure on them, and eventually the federal government redrew them. In addition, many members of tribes were not inclined to remain within the boundaries of a reservation.

By the 1880s, it had become clear that the fate of tribes on reservations resembled that of all the tribes that had had regular contact with white settlers since the first contact in America: a decline into poverty and degradation. Instead of becoming symbols of tribal autonomy, the reservations became illustrations of the inability of traditional tribal ways of life to adapt to a society now dominated by whites.

Out of those concerns came a program of allotments, first instituted by the General Allotment Act (commonly known as the Dawes Act) of 1887. Allotment sought to replace the existing uses of land on reservations—tracts of communally owned land with no precise boundaries—with "allotted" land with distinct borders that individual tribal members would own. The allotment program drew on a long association in Anglo-American culture between fee simple ownership and efficient and productive uses of land, prosperity, and independence. By turning from communal ownership and use of land to individual use, proponents of allotment believed, tribe members would become more self-sufficient and prosperous.

While some tribes supported allotment, most were unenthusiastic. Tribes pointed out that their communal uses of land were not inconsistent with productivity, that they were not interested in abandoning their traditional tribal ways for those of white American society, and that they were fearful that tribal fee simple ownership would tempt unscrupulous whites to purchase more tribal lands.

The allotment program was nonetheless implemented, and that fact illustrated a reorientation of the federal government's relationship with tribes. A case that demonstrated that development, *Lone Wolf v. Hitchcock*, was decided by the Supreme Court in 1903. The Kiowa-Comanche tribe challenged allotment legislation allowing the federal government to acquire land within that tribe's reservation and allot it to tribal members, without securing the consent of three-fourths of the adult members of the tribe, as required by an 1867 treaty between the tribe and the United States. The tribe argued that the legislation violated the treaty and did not provide adequate compensation for the tribe, in violation of the just compensation clause of the Fifth Amendment.

In *Lone Wolf*, a unanimous Court reframed tribal relations with the federal government and legitimated the allotment program. Building on *Johnson v. McIntosh*'s characterization of tribes as "domestic dependent" nations, the Court held that since the federal government could nullify treaties with foreign nations in the national interest, it could do the same with tribal treaties. The power of the United States to abrogate treaties did not rest on any provision of the Constitution but on the need of a sovereign state to preserve itself. And since the federal government, through Congress, was the sole institution charged with exercising authority over tribes, and its relationship with the tribes paralleled that of guardian to ward, its decisions affecting the tribes were insulated from judicial review. With *Lone Wolf*, the last jurisprudential obstacle to the federal government taking tribal land was removed.

Recent history

By the 1930s, white humanitarians who had favored allotment had concluded that on the whole, tribes were no more assimilated, no more prosperous, and no more inclined to embrace settler-type forms of agriculture than they had been in the 1880s. In fact, one newspaper editorialized in 1934 that the allotment policy had "destroyed the native society, economy and organization." In 1934, Congress ended allotments with the Indian Reorganization Act. Reservations remained in place, and the Bureau of Indian Affairs was authorized to restore to tribes all the land on reservations that had been transferred to the federal government but not allotted or sold to whites. The system in place before 1887 was restored, but without all the sold or parceled-out land.

Although Congress has wanted to get out of the business of entering into treaties with tribes since 1870, numerous treaties remain in place. With the end of the allotment program, tribes began to draw attention to violations of those treaties and other unauthorized seizures of tribal land that had occurred before *Lone Wolf*. Twenty-first-century courts have listened. In a 2001 decision, the Cayuga Nation in New York received an award of $248 million for portions of their land that New York state had seized illegally in 1795 and 1807. The standard the court applied in evaluating New York's actions was the governing relations between tribes and states in the late eighteenth and early nineteenth centuries.

One can thus anticipate that the consistent pattern of eighteenth- and nineteenth-century white settlers depriving tribes of their land may actually help tribes retrieve some of that land. For it is clear that even though the initial proposition that tribes were regarded as the "owners" of land they occupied in early America was regularly ignored in practice, it remains a source of legal authority for contemporary tribal land claims. One of the ironies of the legal history of American Indian tribes is that the long-standing disregard by both white settlers and American governmental institutions of the rights and interests of tribes has emerged as a basis for restoring those rights and interests in the twenty-first century.

Chapter 2
Law and African American slavery

Two dominant themes of American history from the colonial years to the outbreak of the Civil War involved the subjugation of ethnic minorities within the American population. The legal and social treatment of American Indians and African American slaves in America was unique. Other nations, all over the world, have histories that include the subjugation and exploitation of aboriginal peoples and the legitimation of the institution of slavery. Only the United States, however, forged its identity as a nation devoted to the natural rights principles of liberty and equality while treating its Indian and African American residents as unequal persons ineligible for the full range of liberties.

As with the exploitation of indigenous tribes, African American slavery helped foster the population growth, expansion of the labor force, extraction of abundant agricultural resources, and commercial prosperity that seemed to make the United States a singularly favored nation in the first half of the nineteenth century. African American slavery, however, had independent significance: it was the root cause of the breakup of that nation in 1860 and the civil war that accompanied it.

The colonial heritage of slavery in America

By the time of American independence, slavery in the United States had taken on regional dimensions, with the vast majority of slaves residing in the South. Slavery had also become, in practice, nearly exclusively confined to persons of African descent. Finally, slavery had become a controversial sectional issue, with some northern states considering the emancipation of slaves. None of those characteristics of American slavery were fully present in its earlier history.

The practice of slavery was not controversial in any of the colonies before the eighteenth century. Slavery was universally accepted among the nations that participated in colonial settlement, which included some African kingdoms as well as those in Europe. Slavery was a status traditionally associated with being a captive in war, and the slave populations on the American continent were made up of individuals whose tribes had been conquered in wars in North America or in Africa. Slavery in North America was not confined to persons of African descent: initially most of the slaves owned by Spanish colonists in North America came from conquered populations of Indians. Eventually, American colonies would equate slave status with African descent, but that process did not get under way until the eighteenth century.

Bondsmen, as slaves were originally called, were just one group of persons with servile status in the American colonies. Other groups included indentured servants, who were bound to their masters for a specific term of years, and apprentices, persons attached to tradesmen who were taught trades in exchange for their services. Historians have characterized the early American colonies as "societies with slaves," in which slavery was merely one species of servile labor relationships, rather than "slave societies," in which slavery was a dominant economic and social institution.

Although 90 percent of the slaves in America from the opening of the eighteenth century to independence resided in southern colonies, slavery was practiced in all of the colonies, and efforts to emancipate slaves did not surface in any northern colonies until after independence. Restrictions on slaves' conduct, such as being forbidden to be in public after dark or to travel without passes, were widespread in southern colonies and not uncommon in northern colonies. In both the North and the South, similar restrictions were placed on other persons with servile status and on members of marginal populations, such as American Indians.

The use of law to determine slave status and regulate slaves' actions was not uniform throughout the colonies. Some colonies, notably southern ones with sizable slave populations, promulgated "slave codes," collections of laws regulating the civil and criminal conduct of slaves. Slave codes designated persons' eligibility to be held in slavery and regulated the conduct of masters and other members of the white population, setting terms for the emancipation of slaves and providing penalties for people who encouraged slaves to escape or sheltered those who did.

In some colonies, slave codes were not employed. But in all colonies, two other legal regimes governed the practice of slavery: legislative provisions designed to control and punish "disorderly" conduct among servile or marginal populations, and the informal common law of slavery, which gave slave masters widespread discretion to regulate and punish the slaves they owned. When slave populations in a colony grew to a critical mass, that colony typically enacted a slave code and created special slave courts where offenses by slaves could be tried. Although enslaved persons were not typically permitted to testify in the ordinary courts of a colony, their testimony was permitted in the slave courts. In most cases, it was disadvantageous to slave-owners to have their slaves executed for crimes—masters were typically entitled to compensation when that occurred—or to have them incarcerated for long periods. Thus, one of the functions of slave courts was to impose punishments other than death or extended incarceration. The typical punishment was physical: whippings, beatings, and in some instances castration. Another option, employed for "incorrigibles," was deportation to another slave colony, where a slave could be sold without the disclosure of past criminal offenses.

Between 1700 and 1780, the number of slaves in colonial America grew from approximately 30,000 to approximately 450,000, with 90 percent residing in southern colonies. In that time frame, colonies with sizable numbers of slaves began to limit eligibility for slave status to persons of African descent, to restrict owners' emancipation of slaves, and to assure the generational transfer of slave status by equating slavery with the condition of a child's mother. More colonies in the South (and eventually the North) passed slave codes, and increased numbers of the white population were enlisted to enforce those codes, a process that culminated in the emergence in most southern cities and towns of "slave patrols" composed of both nonslaveholders and slaveholders. Slave patrols were responsible for ensuring that slaves did not escape outside the borders of a colony or engage in behavior that was deemed rebellious or otherwise a threat to authority. When slaves traveled outside the company of their masters, they were required to have "papers" on their persons that identified them and their masters and sometimes granted them permission to make the journey. Such papers were routinely inspected by slave patrols.

These changes reflected the eighteenth-century transformation of some southern colonies into slave societies. Importation of slaves into those colonies continued at a rapid pace, and slave-owners encouraged procreation among their slave populations to add to their stock of slaves. Staple-crop plantation agriculture, which relied on the use of slave labor to plant, harvest, and process crops such as tobacco, rice, and indigo for domestic and European markets, became the principal form of economic activity in these colonies. Plantations became self-sufficient economic units that used slave labor in a variety of capacities, ranging from domestic tasks to handicrafts. Successful plantations were able to provide household sustenance from their

2. A slave auction in the South. When the image appeared in *Harper's Weekly* in July 1861, the Civil War was in its fourth month, and slavery was still flourishing in some areas of the South. President Abraham Lincoln would not issue the Emancipation Proclamation until September 1862.

own crops, produce specialized goods to sell in domestic markets, and market most of their staple crops to Europe. In exchange, they imported luxury goods from Europe, which they paid for with credit that European merchants advanced them on the basis of their projected seasonal crop outputs. Slave labor was thus the economic basis of plantation life.

By the outset of the Revolutionary War, the stage was set for a potential reexamination of slavery in the new American nation. First, the future profitability of slavery became clouded as some southern colonies with sizable slave populations, such as Maryland and Virginia, experienced the exhaustion of soil suitable for growing their principal staple crop, tobacco. In those colonies, plantations based on slave labor had become less ubiquitous. Meanwhile, the war created incentives for both sides to recruit African Americans to their causes, and emancipation became a way of attracting potential recruits. As enlistments in the war reduced the size of slave patrols, it became more difficult to keep large slave populations in check in southern colonies.

Finally, the natural rights ideology that helped propel American independence provided an obvious contrast with the practice of slavery. Thomas Jefferson recognized that contrast in an omitted section of the 1776 draft of the Declaration of Independence. Aware of the contradiction between slaveholding and natural rights, Jefferson had sought to include, in his list of grievances against King George III of Great Britain that formed the Declaration's principal justification for independence, British participation in the international slave trade. Perhaps Jefferson intended to blame the British, who had abolished slavery in England, for tempting American colonials to become slave-owners. If so, his effort failed. Delegates from Georgia and South Carolina to the Continental Congress forced the deletion of the slave trade reference in the Declaration's final version.

Slavery and the Constitution

In the years between the Declaration and the first decade of the nineteenth century, several states, all of them in the North, abolished slavery. Vermont was first to do so in 1777, followed by Massachusetts and Pennsylvania (1780), Rhode Island and Connecticut (1784), New York (1799), and New Jersey (1804). In addition, both Maryland and Virginia debated emancipation, and in 1782 Virginia removed most of its restrictions on manumission (the formal freeing of slaves), which resulted in a significant increase of freed African Americans there.

The differing regional trends affecting slavery in the years after independence set the stage for the eventual treatment of slavery by the framers of the Constitution. When the first document creating a federal union of states, the Articles of Confederation, was ratified in 1781, its article IV provided that the "privileges and immunities" of residents of the new states would extend only to free persons, and its article IX prohibited Congress, the unicameral federal government, from making treaties affecting the import or export of "any species of goods or commodities whatsoever." When taken along with the very limited powers assigned to the federal government in article II, those provisions ensured that slavery would be a question of state law.

After the Revolutionary War ended with the Treaty of Paris in 1783, the British relinquished all their claims to land east of the Mississippi, which became territory owned by the new government of the United States. In 1787, the Articles government enacted the Northwest and Southwest Ordinances, which divided the former British territory into two portions, with the Ohio River serving as a boundary, and provided rules for the portions. The Northwest Ordinance abolished slavery in territorial lands north of the Ohio River; the Southwest Ordinance was silent on the subject. Article VI of the Northwest Ordinance provided that any runaway slaves captured north of the Ohio River would be returned to their masters.

There matters stood when the delegates at the 1787 Philadelphia convention drafted the Constitution of the United States, replacing the federal government created by the Articles of Confederation with a new one. The framers of the Constitution treated this new federal government as one having limited powers that were enumerated in the Constitution's text. If a power was not expressly given to the federal government, it remained in the states. None of the federal government's enumerated powers in the Constitution included a power to regulate slavery, which meant that decisions to abolish or retain slavery were under the authority of the states. But a clause in the Constitution provided that the federal government could determine the status of slavery in federal territories that had not yet joined the Union. Article IV, section 3 of the Constitution gave the new federal Congress the power "to . . . make all needful rules and regulations respecting the Territory . . . belonging to the United States." That was initially understood to include rules about slavery, so the Northwest and Southwest Ordinances were assumed to remain in effect.

Although the Constitution did not use the word "slavery," several of its provisions acknowledged slavery's existence. Article I, section 2, in the course of apportioning representatives in the lower house of Congress, distinguished between "free Persons, including those bound to Service for a Term of Years," and "all other persons," who were to be counted as three-fifths of "free Persons." Article IV, section 2 (the "fugitive slave clause"), stated: "No Person held to Service or Labour in one State, under the Laws thereof, escaping into another, shall, in Consequence of any Law or Regulation therein, be discharged from such Service or Labour, but shall be delivered up on Claim of the Party to whom such Service or Labour may be due." Another section of article IV reinforced the fugitive slave clause by providing: "Full Faith and Credit shall be given in each State to the public Acts, Records, and judicial Proceedings of every other state."

The other references to slavery in the Constitution involved the international slave trade. Article I, section 9, clause 1 provided that "the Migration or Importation of such Persons as any of the States now existing shall think proper to admit shall not be prohibited by the Congress prior to [1808]." And article V (which addressed amendments to the Constitution) provided that "no Amendment which shall be made prior to [1808] shall in any Manner affect the first and fourth Clauses in the Ninth Section of the first Article." Those clauses fixed the ratio of a state's population to the taxes it paid to the federal government, so article V, looking ahead to the possible abolition of the international slave trade in 1808, assured that until that year slaves would continue to be counted as three-fifths of other persons for the purposes of determining a state's tax obligations.

Several delegates to the 1787 convention from slaveholding states had become concerned that if northern states continued their pattern of immediate or gradual emancipation and the slave trade were abolished, future Congresses might be composed of more free states than slave states, and the slave populations of the latter might level off or decline. This would reduce the aggregate number of slave state representatives in Congress and increase the aggregate number of free state representatives.

In sum, the treatment of slavery in the 1787 Constitution illustrates the framers' decision to acknowledge, but not trumpet, its presence and reveals the concerns of representatives of slave-owning states about its future. At the time of the Constitution's framing, beliefs were widely shared among members of the framing generation that slavery was an awkward phenomenon in a nation ostensibly founded on natural rights principles and could be expected to die out sometime in the future, but that the timing and consequences of this event were unpredictable and potentially calamitous for some states in the Union.

Slavery and regional conflict (1800–1860)

Over the first half of the nineteenth century, a series of factors combined to make slavery a more profitable and expansive economic activity than the framers had contemplated and at the same time a distinctly regional one. Consequently, the increasingly contentious issue of slave ownership was propelled into the center of American politics.

The territory of the American nation vastly expanded between 1800 and 1860. By purchasing or conquering territory from Spain, France, Mexico, and Great Britain, the United States more than doubled its size in that time period. Settlers from coastal states began to migrate westward into federal territories, and the federal government initiated the policy of Indian removal. Between 1798 and 1820, the states of Kentucky, Tennessee, Ohio, Louisiana, Indiana, Missouri, and Maine had entered the Union. All but Maine were carved out of western lands included in the

Louisiana Purchase of 1803 or ceded to the federal government by Virginia and North Carolina in the 1780s. By the 1830s, the tribes remaining in new federal territories had ceded their land to allow the formation of several new states, including Alabama, Mississippi, and Illinois.

Law had thus facilitated territorial expansion and white settlers' occupation of new territories. Then, as territorial expansion was under way, a development occurred that suggested that some of the new territories were likely to include slave populations. Cotton emerged as a new, potentially profitable staple crop that could be grown in the American South. The marketability of cotton was a function of the invention of the cotton gin, a machine that separated the seeds of coarser cotton plants from their fibers, and the associated growth of textile mills, where machine operators could produce cotton garments out of the fibers. Delicate cotton, with longer fibers, could not be grown outside the coastal regions of the lower South, and was thus not a promising staple crop, but coarser cotton plants could survive in drier, cooler environments. Once cotton gins became available, cotton planting became a dominant form of agriculture in the new federal territories that would become Alabama, Mississippi, Louisiana, and Arkansas. Given the worldwide demand for relatively cheap, durable cotton clothing, growing cotton appeared to be a highly profitable enterprise.

Planting, growing, and harvesting cotton were labor-intensive activities, ideally suited for cheap labor, slavery being the cheapest form. As the United States acquired territory suitable for cotton production in the trans-Appalachian south, settlers and their slaves poured into the region, eventually forming the basis of new states. In the same time period, established states began to subsidize the construction of turnpikes, bridges, and canals to link northern coastal areas to the states carved out of federal territories in the Ohio Valley and Great Lakes regions. Both of those developments facilitated western migration both north and south of the Ohio River. Many of the people moving west were immigrants from Europe who had been welcomed by U.S. immigration policies designed to increase the American labor force. But because slave labor was entrenched in agricultural regions in the South, most European immigrants sought work in the Northeast and Midwest, where the agricultural and industrial labor markets were wage based.

In 1800, approximately 387,000 persons lived west of the states bordering the Atlantic coast. By 1810 that number had reached nearly 1,400,000 and by 1820 about 2,500,000. The migration of settlers westward continued in the succeeding decades, and by 1860 half the American population lived west of the Appalachians. By the 1850s, sizable American settlements had been established in California and Oregon Territory, and Americans in both the North and the South expected the patterns of westward migration eventually to continue throughout the trans-Mississippi west to the Pacific coast.

Thus, as the American population grew and moved westward in the first half of the nineteenth century, it became clear that the slave economy was capable of sustaining itself, even thriving. At the same time, it appeared that it would remain a distinctly regional phenomenon. As new states joined the Union in the 1840s, a decade when cotton-based plantation agriculture had become commonplace, the new southwestern states had a majority of residents who had come from slave states, and they endorsed the practice of slavery. In contrast, every new northern state entering the Union after 1820 had abolished slavery. Although a vast area of relatively flat land stretching from Ohio to the western borders of Iowa and Minnesota seemed ideally suited for staple-crop agriculture, and by the 1850s the area had already become the nation's leading supplier of corn and wheat, its only pockets of slavery were on federal army bases. Moreover, California and Oregon, which entered the Union in the decade of the 1850s, had climates and topographies well suited to staple-crop agriculture but had abolished slavery as well.

The developments just described resulted in two regional economies, one based on slavery and the other on wage earnings, being in place by the third decade of the nineteenth century. It was inevitable that the continued expansion, and potential clash, of these economies would become a divisive issue for American legal institutions. Unfortunately, in the years between 1820 and 1860, none of those institutions was able to forge a satisfactory response to the issue.

Between 1820 and 1857, Congress made a determined effort to ensure that territorial expansion did not disturb sectional equilibrium on slavery. In legislation enacted during these years, Congress outlawed slavery in federal territories north of Missouri's southern border; declined to outlaw slavery in the southern regions of the territory won in the Mexican War; insisted (until 1850) that a precise balance between slave and free states be preserved in the Union; and eventually allowed "unorganized" federal territories (those without a sufficient population to apply for statehood) to choose whether to permit slavery or not. With each of those efforts, sectional tension escalated. By the 1860 election, both of the major parties, the Democrats and Whigs, had fractured on the slavery issue.

While Congress was struggling with the implications of the western expansion of slavery in the 1830s and 1840s, another element was escalating that tension: the growth of abolitionist sentiment in the North. Abolitionists called for the eradication of slavery everywhere in America and encouraged northern states to pass "personal liberty" laws, which granted freedom to escaped slaves who became residents of those states. The laws were in direct conflict with a newly strengthened federal law, the Fugitive Slave Act of 1850, which required persons in free states to help return escaped slaves to their owners.

Fugitive slaves were not only symbols of the increasingly polarized responses to slavery in the 1840s and 1850s; they were litigants in cases that put pressure on legal principles designed to preserve the coexistence of slave and nonslave regions in the federal union. The two leading coexistence principles were the constitutional understanding that slavery in the states was exclusively a matter of state law, and the principle of comity—embodied in the Constitution's Full Faith and Credit Clause—that states would recognize the legal doctrines of other states, including those governing slavery. Until the 1830s, northern states tacitly permitted slaveholders to bring slaves with them on visits without affecting the slaves' status, and southern courts granted freedom to slaves whose masters had taken them to free states and established domiciles in those states. By the 1840s, however, northern courts began to treat slaves who had accompanied their masters to northern states as free, even if the residency had been temporary and domicile had not been established.

This treatment seemed to invite slaves to escape from slave states to free states, where they might be granted freedom on arrival. Fearing that large numbers of slaves in states bordering free states would attempt to escape, southern courts invoked the common law doctrines of "reattachment" and "reversion," which they applied to slaves who had traveled into free states with their masters and then returned to their home states. Under these doctrines, all slaves reentering slave states lost their freedom. The 1857 case of *Dred Scott v. Sandford*, in which the Supreme Court tried to render a definitive judgment on the constitutional status of slavery, was a product of the reattachment and reversion doctrines.

Dred Scott, the slave of Dr. John Emerson, an army surgeon from Missouri, accompanied Emerson on tours of duty to Wisconsin Territory and the free state of Illinois in the 1830s and then returned to Missouri after Emerson married and took up residence in St. Louis. After Emerson's death in 1843, his wife, Eliza, inherited Scott, and he continued to work for her until 1846. That year, he sued for his freedom in a Missouri court, relying on earlier

Missouri cases holding that slaves who had spent time in free states or territories were entitled to their freedom.

Scott's suit was delayed until 1850, when a Missouri trial court declared him free. In the interim, Eliza Emerson had remarried, left Missouri, and entrusted her business affairs to her brother, John Sanford. In order to avoid paying the wages Scott claimed for his services to Eliza Emerson, Sanford appealed the trial court decision to the Missouri Supreme Court. That court reversed its earlier position on slaves reentering Missouri from free states or territories, applied the reattachment doctrine to Scott, and declared him a slave.

Scott's lawyers sought to bring his case before the U.S. Supreme Court by filing a new suit for his freedom in federal court. In response, Sanford's lawyers raised two explosive issues: whether Scott, being an African American, was a "citizen of the United States," eligible to sue in federal court and whether Congress's abolition of slavery in federal territories was an unconstitutional violation of the due process clause of the Fifth Amendment, which prevented the federal government from summarily depriving persons of their property.

In 1857, a divided Supreme Court ruled against Scott on both issues. The opinion of the Court, written by Chief Justice Roger Taney, first announced that because African Americans had been regarded as a "degraded class" of persons at the time of independence and slaves had never been treated as citizens of states, they would not be treated as citizens of the United States. Scott was thus not eligible to bring a suit in the federal courts. Taney then went on to declare—although his finding that Scott could not sue in the federal courts made the declaration unnecessary—that the portion of the Missouri Compromise that outlawed slavery in some federal territories was unconstitutional. Both pronouncements were of dubious validity. Several states had made free blacks citizens in the late eighteenth century, and in the 1820 debate over the Missouri Compromise both sides had assumed that Congress had the power to ban slavery in territories.

Dred Scott was immediately attacked by antislavery advocates in Congress and elsewhere. In the 1860 presidential election, the Republican Party platform declared that the constitutionality of slavery in the federal territories had not been definitively decided in the case and pledged to oppose any efforts to introduce slavery into those territories. Despite the Court's effort, *Dred Scott* had not been able to defuse sectional tension over slavery and westward expansion. The decision can be seen as the culmination of six decades in which American legal institutions sought to ameliorate sectional conflict over slavery and instead exacerbated it. A civil war would be necessary to end slavery in America and forcibly restore a union of northern and southern states. Even that cataclysmic event, and the subsequent abolition of slavery in the Thirteenth Amendment to the Constitution (1865) would not remove the legacy of slavery from its central—and polarizing—place in U.S. history. The legacy of slavery would survive in the form of pervasive discrimination against African Americans.

Chapter 3
Rights of property and their regulation

From the first European contacts with the American continent, property rights and their relationship to government were foundational legal issues. One reason was timing. The societies from which the first European voyagers came had abandoned feudal conceptions of property ownership, so that the ownership of property by individuals, especially property in land, had come to be thought of as a highly valuable social asset. Another reason was the abundance of "undeveloped" land and the shortage of agricultural labor in America, which made land comparatively easy for settlers to acquire and, if European settlements expanded, a commodity that could be traded in markets. A final reason was the strong need, immediately recognized by settlers, to have some governmental structure for allocating land and identifying landownership. The law of real property (land and substances permanently attached to it) and, to a lesser extent, personal property was thus at the very center of early American society and governance.

Land, labor, and government in early America

Although the first European settlers of North America came from several countries, English settlement and the legacy of English common law soon came to dominate the treatment of property issues in America. This resulted in a recurrent pattern of developments: traditional English practices involving the ownership and transfer of property, and traditional English forms of agricultural labor, were modified in the distinctive setting of the American British colonies.

Landownership in seventeenth- and eighteenth-century England was concentrated in a small number of families who handed down ownership from generation to generation. The limited availability of open land in England and the persistence of hierarchical social arrangements made it extremely difficult for persons below the nobility and gentry classes to alter their status from tenant to landowner. One of the principal reasons low-status residents of England began to migrate to the American colonies in the 1600s was the opportunity to acquire land for themselves.

The American colonies posed a sharp contrast to England in the ratio of available land to the labor force. Although tracts of land were plentiful and comparatively cheap in America, their "cultivation"—transformation into enclosed spaces sufficient for producing crops and goods capable of sustaining a household and being marketed—required agricultural labor, which itself required a critical mass of population. From the earliest American settlements, the conversion of land into a profitable commodity was dependent on a significant growth of the colonial labor force.

Those characteristics of landholding in early America were to have major effects on the law of property rights and their regulation. One illustration was the flourishing of African slavery in America even after slavery had been abolished in England. The importation of African slaves into the southern coastal colonies and the emergence in those colonies of staple crop plantation agriculture featuring slave labor were responses to the easy availability of large tracts of land in the South that could produce staple, marketable crops and the shortage of agricultural laborers. Over time, the establishment of slave labor in southern colonies created disincentives for other categories of European agricultural laborers—indentured servants, apprentices, and wage laborers—to emigrate to those colonies. They came instead to the northern and middle colonies, where they sought through the acquisition of land to escape their status as servants, apprentices, and tenants as rapidly as possible.

By the late eighteenth century, as colonial Americans had become independent of the British Empire, a set of "creole elites"—third-generation residents of America whose families had accumulated wealth and acquired high social status through agricultural householding and associated mercantile pursuits—had emerged throughout the colonies. Many of those families were one generation removed from ancestors who had bought tracts of recently surveyed land and sold them at a profit. These elites had come to conceive of freehold landownership in the traditional English fashion, as an index of social and economic power.

As landownership and forms of labor evolved in early America, so did the role of law in identifying, allocating, and regulating property ownership and use. One of the earliest symbols of land use regulation were the recording acts passed by colonial legislatures. Those acts prescribed procedures for surveying and recording tracts of land as part of claiming title to them. Deeds specified the boundaries of the land and asserted title to it. In most colonies, the first person to record a deed to land at a local courthouse was treated as the owner of the land, even if a competing claimant could produce an earlier unrecorded deed.

Recording acts reflected the strong desire of colonial townships to encourage their members to acquire land that could be cultivated. And as townships became established, they regulated the use of property in numerous other ways. They required buildings to be constructed of stone and brick to prevent fires, the streets adjacent to homes to be cleaned by the homeowners, and the slaughter of animals to be confined to particular areas. Other governing institutions in the colonies regulated the ownership and use of property. They granted bounties of land to stimulate the production of certain goods, such as hemp, potash, and tar. They occasionally awarded special patents to inventors and franchises to transportation ventures such as bridges and ferries. They claimed the power to take property for public uses by eminent domain, gradually establishing a practice of paying compensation to the owners. In short, by the opening of the nineteenth century, life in America had become synonymous with the acquisition and use of property and with governmental restrictions on that acquisition and use.

The antebellum period

In the first half of the nineteenth century, American institutions considered the relationship of private property to government regulation in a context of dramatic population growth and territorial expansion, coupled with a strong demand for increased transportation and a shortage of investment capital. States and the federal government became promoters of economic development, engaging in land sales, financing transportation projects, and creating corporate franchises whose operations they both subsidized and sought to regulate.

By the middle of the nineteenth century, both federal and state courts had established the principle that all contractual arrangements were undertaken against the backdrop of a state's eminent domain power, along with the principle that when property was taken through eminent domain, some form of compensation needed to be paid. Courts and legal commentators continued to identify protection of property as one of the foundational principles of American jurisprudence, but at the same time the regulation of property by governmental institutions proceeded apace. Although it was clear that legislatures could not take property from one citizen and give it to another without some form of legal process or seize property under eminent domain powers without paying some compensation, property rights were by no means inviolate. Courts justified interferences with established franchise holdings of turnpike, bridge, or canal companies on behalf of competitors whose operations were seen as "improvements." At the outbreak of the Civil War, property rights remained largely subject to governmental regulation in the perceived interest of the community at large.

Property rights, Reconstruction, and the late nineteenth-century economy

With the elimination of slavery, the reunification of the nation, and the emergence of large-scale industrial enterprises, such as railroads, manufacturers, and the holding companies associated with them, the stage was set for the gradual replacement of American agricultural householding with an interdependent, nationally oriented industrialized economy. These developments would take place in an altered legal landscape.

Prior to the Civil War, the federal government undertook comparatively little regulation of property. After Reconstruction the government began to do so, but not primarily in the person of Congress or the executive. Instead, the federal judiciary began interpreting the due process clause of the newly ratified Fourteenth Amendment (1867) to define the boundary between the police powers of the states and private property rights. Although those decisions are outside the scope of this book, their cumulative effect on regulatory legislation is worthy of note: the courts' generally tolerant posture toward that legislation changed, and they began to approach it skeptically, mindful of its potentially redistributive effects. That same judicial stance also emerged in late nineteenth-century decisions interpreting the scope of federal power to regulate interstate commerce. For example, when Congress, in the Interstate Commerce Act of 1887 and the Sherman Anti-Trust Act of 1891, sought to regulate the railroad industry and prohibit mergers and acquisitions that tended to retard competition, the Supreme Court determined

3. This poster advertised a sheriff's sale of a house and barn, together with an acre and a half of land, to take place on February 4, 1880, in Newtown Township, Bucks County, Pennsylvania. The poster describes the buildings and notes that the properties had been seized from John B. Kephart as part of a foreclosure proceeding. Such foreclosure sales have been a long-standing basis of transferring real property in America and remain so today.

for itself whether common carrier rates set by regulators were "reasonable" and whether mergers or acquisitions were anticompetitive. The Court construed federal commerce powers narrowly, distinguishing regulations on "commerce," which it found constitutionally permissible, from those on "manufacture" or "production," which it found were not.

In the same time period, however, the Court engrafted a "police power exception" to legislation affecting existing contracts that permitted legislatures to modify the terms of their prior contractual arrangements on grounds of public health, safety, or morals. When the twentieth century opened, the jurisprudence of property rights and their regulation stood in a quite different position from that at the opening of the Civil War. The altered posture has been variously described by legal and constitutional historians; perhaps the best way to understand it is to recognize that "property rights," long treated in American culture as foundational to free republican governments but at the same time potentially subservient to these governments' needs, had become a legal term of art. The boundary between public power and private rights would now be traced by the judiciary.

The transformation of property rights jurisprudence (1900–1940)

Only four decades after that altered conception of the relationship between property rights and regulatory government had become orthodoxy, it was significantly altered. In the years between 1900 and 1940, an increased amount of state legislation regulating property was sustained by courts, and the federal government emerged as an important agent of regulation. This development took place in a time period when the assumption that market solutions to the distribution of property should be left undisturbed by government was called into question and when an American economy based on largely unregulated capitalism underwent a severe depression. Both state and federal regulatory legislation sought to respond to the economic crisis, and eventually the judiciary tolerated that intervention.

For the first three decades of the twentieth century, courts continued to be involved with tracing the boundary between the public welfare and private rights and delineating the scope of federal and state power to regulate interstate commerce. The framework in which property rights challenges to legislation came to the U.S. Supreme Court resembled that of the previous century, but the amount of legislation dramatically increased, especially after 1930.

In property rights cases in which judges engaged in boundary tracing, they saw themselves less as antagonists or supporters of economic reform, or defenders or critics of business interests, than as guardians of both the legislative process and private property. An increasing number of critics of judicial decisions, however, took a different view. To them, these decisions reflected inappropriate substitutions of the economic views of unelected judges for more publicly accountable institutions: Congress and state legislatures.

By the early twentieth century, a number of legal commentators and some judges had come to emphasize the indeterminacy and shifting meaning of many legal provisions and concluded that instead of "law" remaining independent of the decisions of its interpreters, it was synonymous with their interpretations. This meant that once one assumed that judges were as inclined to have partisan ideological agendas as any other group of humans, judicial decisions, like other forms of law in America, could be seen as reflecting such agendas.

It followed, for those critics, that since many judges were appointed officials with life tenure, their decisions were subjected to fewer direct political checks than those of elected officials, and therefore they should hesitate to substitute their interpretations of constitutional provisions for the views of legislative majorities.

This meant that when legislation regulating property or redistributing economic benefits was challenged on constitutional or other legal grounds, judges should be loath to substitute their particular views on the efficacy of the legislation for those of popularly elected decision-makers.

In the first three decades of the twentieth century, this debate about the proper stance of the U.S. Supreme Court in reviewing legislation on constitutional grounds was largely confined to academics. But once the American economy entered into an extended depression at the opening of the 1930s, some states and Congress made several efforts to pass legislation that placed restrictions on private economic activity. When the Roosevelt administration introduced legislation creating federal agencies to regulate industry and agriculture, sought to compel the mortgagors of distressed farmers to relinquish portions of their mortgages, and used the commerce power to regulate labor relations in the coal industry, the Court struck down that legislation on constitutional grounds. Between 1934 and 1937, the Court struck down more federal legislation affecting property rights than in any previous period in American history.

By 1940, however, a combination of factors had resulted in the Court assuming a far more deferential attitude toward federal and state legislation regulating economic activity or redistributing economic benefits. Part of the Court's revised attitude came from a recognition by some justices that strict constitutional limitations on economic regulation could amount to a subsidy to employers that might have deleterious effects in depressed economic conditions. Another part came from changes in personnel on the Court. Finally, yet another part came from the tacit recognition within the judiciary of the arguments about unchecked "lawmaking" by judges in a majoritarian democracy. All of those factors eventually produced a new standard of judicial review of legislation regulating property rights, one resting on a presumption that such legislation was legally justifiable if a rational basis for it could be discerned. By the time the United States entered World War II in 1941, judicial deference to legislation regulating property rights had become the norm.

The contemporary jurisprudence of property rights

American economic thought took a turn toward unregulated markets after the 1980s, and appointments to the Court between the 1970s and the close of the century were primarily made by Republican presidents. But the Court's constitutional jurisprudence of cases involving the regulation of property remained largely intact. The Court's attitude toward regulatory takings and legislative modification of existing private contractual agreements remained permissive: in one case, a majority of the Court allowed a city to use its eminent domain power to further private development, suggesting that there were virtually no limits on the exercise of the power.

Meanwhile, as developments in digital technology increased, the forms of intellectual property, the category of "property" expanded in the latter years of the twentieth century, and the traditional legal categories of intellectual property, patents, copyrights, trademarks, and trade secrets were placed under pressure. Congress and the courts both struggled to adopt existing legal rules to this new intellectual property environment.

In 1984, the Supreme Court ruled that trade secrets should be considered "property" under the Fifth Amendment's compensation clause but left open the question whether the same applied to patents. Meanwhile, the U.S. Court of Appeals for the Federal Circuit, the court charged with overseeing the process of patent applications, broadened the scope of protection for existing patents, and the Supreme Court, concerned about the effects of those rulings on competition and innovation, tightened the standards for granting new patents. In the same period, copyright protection became an increasingly visible issue. In 1998, Congress extended the duration of existing copyrights to seventy years after the deaths of their authors, and the Court upheld that legislation.

Policy-makers did not respond to the growth of the Internet with regulation. Among the barriers to regulation were the difficulty of enforcing regulations in an intellectual property market that crossed national as well as state boundaries, the ease with which participants could post information anonymously, and the speed with which the content of postings could be altered. The result has been that one of the major potential sources of intellectual property "rights" in the digital age has not yielded either much legal protection for those "rights" or many restrictions on the scope or content of communications on the Internet. Most of the "protection" for Internet-based enterprises has been secured through technology, which in the hands of sophisticated entrepreneurs such as Microsoft or Google has created dominant positions in digital markets through the erection of technical barriers that prevent competitors from duplicating innovations. A defining feature of the massive growth of intellectual property has been its largely unregulated status.

Property rights and their regulation in American history

As a result of the circumstances of life in colonial America, the process of acquiring and using property, especially property in land, took on great social significance. As the American colonies detached themselves from the British Empire, the idea of a class of property owners establishing republican government in the United States emerged as a powerful ingredient of national independence. From the earliest days of American history, "rights" of property were taken as a defining feature of American citizenship.

From the beginnings of colonial settlement as well, however, townships regulated property for the common good. Initially this was because the early settlements in colonial America needed to control land use for their self-preservation. Later it was because the development of the nation rested on the productive distribution of population through vast amounts of space, requiring large-scale transportation projects that were launched and regulated by states. By the early nineteenth century, two ideas about property were coexisting in the property rights cases: the idea that rights of property were inherent in American citizenship and held against state regulation, and the corresponding idea that the police power of the state could regulate property to promote public health, safety, or morals.

For most of American legal history, the opposition of those two ideas was played out in a series of legislative acts and judicial decisions that sought to fix the appropriate boundary between private property rights and the public welfare. Over time, the posture of the states, Congress, and the courts toward the location of that boundary changed, with twentieth-century legislatures progressively regulating economic activity and redistributing economic benefits more fully than their nineteenth-century counterparts, and twentieth-century Supreme Courts unevenly, but progressively, tolerating that regulation. By the close of World War II, legislative restrictions on property rights were common.

Throughout this history, Americans had shown a remarkable capacity for developing new and profitable uses of property, ranging from tracts of land through agricultural and mercantile enterprises, transportation franchises, heavy and light industries, communications networks, and other forms of intellectual property. The deep faith Americans had in the idea of private property had been periodically reinforced by its capacity to generate money. At the same time, the profitability of private enterprise, and the ability of property holders to preserve profits generated from their property for themselves and their progeny, had reinforced social and economic inequalities in America and run counter to the egalitarian ethos that was also a distinctive feature of American culture. Thus, the very success of profitable uses of private property spurred calls for its regulation and for the redistribution of the economic benefits this use produced among the population at large. The result has been a continuous interplay between searches for profitable uses of private property and governmental efforts to ensure that an appropriate share of the resulting profits are put to beneficial public use. The legal history of property rights in America has been shaped by that interplay.

Chapter 4
Law and entrepreneurship

From the origins of European settlement in America, a central concern of those who came to North America was to identify business ventures that would enable them to survive and perhaps to thrive. Over the years Americans have continued to search for profitable activities, and law has figured prominently in that search.

The term "entrepreneurship" refers to the process of creating, launching, and sustaining a business venture in a market-based economy. Different forms of entrepreneurship have been prominent at different times in American history. Through the nineteenth century, the forms consisted of the acquisition of and speculation in land, the populating of the expanded territory of the nation through the development of transportation franchises and the dispersal of public lands, and the nationwide development and distribution of the products of industrial enterprise. In the twentieth and twenty-first centuries, entrepreneurial ventures in communications media, ranging from radio and moving pictures to television and sites on the Internet, have become increasingly prominent.

The colonial and revolutionary years: land acquisition

Each of the British colonial expeditions to North America was the result of a charter from the British Crown to a private company or to the individuals known as the "proprietors" of a colony. Those charters were understood to give their recipients the authority to establish North American settlements by claiming land on behalf of the Crown. Although the Crown's claim to territory whose boundaries it did not know and which had never been inhabited by British subjects was dubious, the first colonial settlers proceeded to claim land in America on behalf of their king and to act as if they "owned" the land on which they settled.

As colonies became established over the course of the seventeenth century, the governing bodies of several colonies, and subsequently individual residents, "bought" tracts of land from adjacent Amerindian tribes, sometimes recording their purchases in treaties or deeds. In most instances, tribes did not understand these transactions as more than agreements to share hunting, fishing, or farming rights on land where they had traditionally engaged in those activities.

Whatever the "sale" of portions of tribal land meant to the tribes, it was clear that European settlers believed that the ownership of land gave its owner exclusive right to its possession and use, so a legal document establishing the ownership of a particular tract associated an owner with a potentially valuable asset. Thus, land grants from the Crown to the proprietors of colonies and from those persons to other individuals, treaties with tribes, and deeds describing the boundaries of land tracts were early steps in the most ubiquitous entrepreneurial activity in seventeenth- and eighteenth-century America: the purchase, cultivation, and sale of land.

Initially, the governing bodies of colonial settlements in New England treated land claimed on behalf of the Crown as owned by the residents of townships in common, with the governing councils allocating portions to individual settlers and their families. It soon became evident in the New England colonies, however, that settlers were able to acquire land from native tribes, that no documents identifying the boundaries of tribal lands existed, and that Crown-engendered grants to land in colonial America could be vast and imprecisely described. To facilitate the secure acquisition of land by settlers, a system for establishing land titles seemed necessary. In response to this need, the American recording system, which would spread throughout the colonies, was created. Recording statutes facilitated both the identification and marking out of land tracts and the acquisition of those tracts by persons in a position to cultivate them.

As colonial settlements expanded, tribes retreated, and more "unsettled" land became identified, settlers able to afford the cost of surveying "vacant" lands often found themselves able to lay claims to larger tracts of land than required for subsistence purposes. The owners of these larger tracts came to use them in two principal ways: as the basis of more extensive agricultural households that sold as well as used the crops they produced and as speculative commodities. In the former capacity, land became the foundation of the agricultural household, the dominant social and economic unit of colonial and revolutionary America (which included staple-crop plantations employing slave labor). In the latter capacity, undeveloped land became an investment, one that could be held, bought, or sold like other investments.

English common law rules for the purchase, sale, lease, and bequest of land combined with the early American recording system to create a class of "freeholders," persons who, by owning unrestricted title to their land, were able to generate income from it in several ways: leasing or selling portions of it to others; producing and selling crops extracted from it with the help of wage or slave labor; or speculating on the potential development of vacant land tracts to which they had recorded title. Over the course of the eighteenth century, many American landowners found one or another of those entrepreneurial uses of land profitable, and English legal rules and practices whose purpose had been to retain the ownership of land in a small number of families, such as primogeniture and entail, were modified to make the transfer of land easier. Primogeniture was the practice by which the eldest son in a family succeeded to all the family's lands on the death of the head of the household (typically that son's father). Entail was the practice of reserving the ownership of land to a male relative outside the immediate family circle. Both practices were designed to keep landholdings in the hands of male family members over generations. Most American colonies and states had abolished primogeniture and entail by the close of the eighteenth century, although landowners could still achieve the same results through wills. The principal effect of the abolition of primogeniture and entail was to make lands available to more members of a family. In this fashion, law contributed to the emergence of agricultural householding and land speculation as common ways of acquiring wealth in early America.

Public lands, western migration, and the transportation sector (1800–1860)

The territory of the United States more than doubled in size between 1803 and 1853. In that period, the United States bought the Louisiana Territory from France and what became the state of Florida from Spain. The nation also annexed in 1845 the Republic of Texas, which had declared its independence from Mexico in 1836, and in 1846 the Republic of California, which had seceded from Mexico earlier that year. That same year, the United States ratified a treaty with Great Britain in which the latter relinquished claims to disputed portions of Oregon Territory south of the forty-ninth parallel of northern latitude.

Mexico protested the Texas annexation, but the United States won the war that arose over the matter and by the terms of the peace treaty "purchased" from Mexico a vast chunk of additional territory. The United States paid $15 million for the land stretching northwest from the Rio Grande River through what would become New Mexico, Arizona, Colorado, Utah, and Nevada. In 1853, the nation paid another $10 million to Mexico for a strip of 30,000 square miles south of the Gila River in what is now New Mexico and Arizona. That land was intended for a transcontinental railroad route that never materialized between Charleston, South Carolina, and San Diego on the Pacific coast.

Thus, by 1853 the existing continental boundaries of the United States were in place. The acquisition of public lands west of the original boundaries of the American republic created a significant opportunity to expand the nation's population and resources. But three things needed to happen for that opportunity to be realized. First, most of the inhabitants of the land west of the Mississippi River, who were Indian tribes, would have to be displaced if settlers of European descent were to occupy the lands. Second, settlers needed to be encouraged to move westward from regions near the Atlantic coast. Finally, transportation facilities had to be established for moving large numbers of people from east to west and for creating contacts between population centers in the West and the East.

Filling the new western territories with critical masses of population was the great American entrepreneurial venture of the first half of the nineteenth century. The venture was a mix of public and private initiatives, involving the federal government, states, and private enterprises, which took place over many decades. By the middle of the nineteenth century it had succeeded, at least from the point of view of settlers of European descent. New population centers had sprung up in the Midwest; turnpikes, canals, and railroads connected the eastern and middle sections of the country; new states had entered or were poised to enter the Union; and states and the federal government were attempting to remove tribes from prospective areas of settlement.

4. A wagon train of men, women, and children moves through the Rocky Mountains on its way to California. This hand-colored engraving was published in 1850, the year when the discovery of gold precipitated an influx of prospective settlers to the state. California would join the Union that year.

Law played a prominent role in each of the developments that facilitated the populating of public lands. Before the federal government could survey and place them up for sale, it needed to "extinguish" any private individuals' outstanding title claims to them. At the time the United States began to acquire substantial federal territories, two sets of private claims to land within them existed. One set rested on grants to individuals from nations that had previously occupied portions of the American continent, such as Great Britain, France, Spain, and Mexico. The other rested on "Indian titles," which we have seen arose out of transactions, many in the form of treaties, in which tribes had sold or given land to private individuals.

Only a minuscule portion of the vast public lands acquired by the United States between 1803 and 1853 was affected by uncertainties about land titles. Grants of land to individuals from foreign nations were rarely recognized in U.S. courts, and Indian titles were also given little weight, primarily because after *Johnson v. McIntosh* they were treated as mere rights of occupancy, superseded when the federal government acquired the land. Thus, in most of the newly acquired federal territory the federal government's title to land tracts was secured, and tracts were surveyed in preparation for sale. The surveying procedure, first created by Congress when it organized the Northwest Territory in 1789, consisted of dividing the public lands eligible for sale into thirty-six-square-mile "townships," subdividing the townships into one-mile square lots, and eventually putting those lots up for public auction.

As the public lands of the United States vastly increased in the early nineteenth century, Congress altered its goals in disposing of them and consequently its disposal process as well. During the eighteenth century, Congress was interested in using the revenues from land sales in the Northwest Territory to retire the nation's debt from the Revolutionary War and set the auction price of public land comparatively high. When the major territorial acquisitions of the early nineteenth century produced a glut of public lands, however, Congress's goal shifted to encouraging individuals to settle on them. As a result, Congress successively altered the process for disposing of public lands between the 1830s and the 1850s, with each alteration making it easier and cheaper for settlers to buy land. By the 1850s, people squatting on federal land that had been surveyed by the federal government could buy it at a low fixed price.

The prospective settlement of public lands was facilitated by a dramatic early nineteenth-century increase in European immigration to America. The population grew by 32 percent in the 1830s and in the 1840s by 35 percent. Much of the increase was brought about by new arrivals from Europe. They were drawn to America in part by expectations that land could be acquired comparatively cheaply there. And it was true that if one managed to get from Europe to the vast new American federal territories, it was within the reach of many people to establish themselves as agricultural householders through the purchase of land.

But for most European immigrants to America, it was initially difficult to buy public land. All passengers from Europe landed on the Atlantic coast, and at the time of the Louisiana Purchase, the conveyances for moving west from there were horse, wagon, or stagecoach on land and canoe, rowboat, or flatboat on water. Most roads were dirt or gravel, often impassable in bad weather. Two significant mountain ranges were located between the Atlantic coast and the Mississippi River, roads could not easily be built across them, and there are not many east-west waterways on the continent. When Henry Clay traveled from his home in Lexington, Kentucky, to sessions of Congress in 1806, the trip took three weeks.

Thus, in order to fill up newly acquired public lands with settlers, transportation was needed to enable large numbers of people, and commerce, to move easily between east and west. By 1867, with the completion of a railroad linking the Atlantic and Pacific coasts, the necessary transportation infrastructure—turnpikes, bridges, canals, and railroads—was in place. The journey Clay made in 1806 had been reduced to four days by train in 1846 and was further reduced in the next decade. A network of railroads and canals connected the Mississippi River and the Great Lakes to the Atlantic coast. Cities such as Cleveland, Detroit, and Chicago emerged in midwestern public land areas because they were located near waterways and railroad lines. Large numbers of people were now able to travel westward, settle on public lands, and maintain contacts with eastern markets.

Law played a vital role in the nineteenth-century development of the transportation sector. Because building a turnpike, bridge, canal, or railroad required a major investment in labor and materials and the venture would not realize any income until the new way was open to traffic, potential investors were unlikely to become involved in transportation projects without subsidies or the ability to prevent competitors from cutting into their profits. The state governments were the entities best suited to provide subsidies to transportation entrepreneurs and to enable them to prevent competition. The turnpikes, bridges, canals, steamboats, and railroads that emerged in the early and middle years of the nineteenth century were products of state-private partnerships or built by states themselves. Bridges, steamboats, and railroads were built by companies that secured exclusive franchises from states, and their projects were financed by state bonds, tax revenues, or stock pledges from state or local governments.

When exclusive franchises were granted, states often retained power to set the rates the franchises charged. In the late 1830s, the Supreme Court held in *Charles River Bridge v. Warren Bridge* that a state that had granted one bridge company an exclusive franchise could subsequently license a competitor, so securing a transportation franchise did not guarantee its owner perpetual protection from competition. Nonetheless, state subsidies continued to finance long-distance transportation ventures for most of the nineteenth century. When overland transportation companies needed rights-of-way for their projects, states and localities exercised their eminent domain powers to secure the land in question. Even when the railroad industry grew sufficiently profitable to allow railway lines to be built mainly with private support, railroads continued to acquire state rights-of-way at low costs.

Canals required more massive start-up costs than railways: canal beds of considerable width and some depth had to be excavated and buttressed to prevent erosion. The state of New York decided to finance the Erie Canal, linking the Great Lakes to the port of New York City, by issuing bonds whose interest was repaid by proceeds from tolls. Construction on the canal began in 1819 and was completed in 1826, ultimately spanning 363 miles. Start-up costs to the state totaled more than $7 million but by 1826 had all been repaid from toll revenues. In the wake of the Erie Canal's success, Ohio, Indiana, Illinois, Connecticut, Massachusetts, Rhode Island, and Pennsylvania all built canals in the late 1820s and 1830s.

These early nineteenth-century developments in the transportation sector eventually affected the legal status of most businesses in America. Initially, the companies engaged in transportation ventures were state-created transportation franchises, whose start-up costs were financed by sales of stock or bonds in the franchises to members of the public. Concerns surfaced about the potential liability of stockholders or bondholders in transportation franchises if they collapsed financially or their activities resulted in injuries to people or goods being transported. If persons owning stock or bonds in a transportation company were treated as partners in that company, they could be made responsible for the payment of the company's debts.

In order to prevent that exposure, states began to allow transportation franchises to register as limited liability corporations rather than partnerships, thereby reducing the exposure of stockholders and bondholders to suit. In the same period when transportation ventures expanded, states passed general incorporation laws, which allowed any company to register itself as a limited liability corporation on payment of a relatively nominal fee. By the 1850s, general incorporation was the rule and special franchising the exception, not only in large-scale transportation projects but in most other business ventures.

In these ways, in the first six decades of the nineteenth century, law played a significant part in the mass movement of both settler populations and commercial traffic into newly acquired western territories by supporting ventures in transportation and helping to create and to protect the corporate entities participating in those ventures. Although those developments contributed to the growing prosperity of the American nation in those decades, they would eventually have some troubling consequences. Most troubling was the fact that by facilitating the opening up of newly acquired western territories for settlement, the policies helped staple-crop plantations reliant on slave labor become established in some areas of them. This meant that instead of slavery dying out as the soil of southern coastal plantations became exhausted, it could survive in western regions suitable for the growth of crops such as cotton. As such, the westward expansion of population and commerce into the new public lands became inextricably linked to the increasingly polarizing issue of slavery.

Law and industrial enterprise (1860–1900)

The dominant forms of entrepreneurial activity in the first half of the nineteenth century—settlement of public lands and ventures in transportation—required active support from states and the federal government, including the network of railroads that emerged across the nation after the Civil War. But once that network was in place, large corporate entities emerged in the private sector, and the emphasis of law shifted toward assisting corporations in establishing market power, protecting their market dominance, and operating efficiently.

In 1862, in the midst of the Civil War, a Congress composed mostly of representatives from northern states appropriated funds to build a transcontinental railroad. Prior to 1850, railroad networks had predominantly been located east of the Mississippi River, but with Mexico's cession of territory at the close of the Mexican War and California's entrance into the Union in 1850, railroads connecting the Midwest to the Pacific coast became a priority. Large portions of these lines were to run through federal territory, so subsidies to companies building the lines needed to come from the federal government. A north-central transcontinental route was chosen, extending west from Omaha in the Nebraska Territory through what would become Wyoming, Utah, and Nevada to Sacramento, California. Two corporations, the Union Pacific and the Central Pacific, received land grants and loans from the federal government to build the line. It was completed in 1869, when the Central Pacific portion, built eastward from Sacramento, joined the Union Pacific portion at Promontory, Utah.

Other transcontinental lines followed. By the 1890s five existed, connecting New Orleans, St. Louis, Duluth, and Chicago to Tacoma, Portland, Sacramento, and Los Angeles. The lines facilitated the access of regions in the trans-Mississippi west to the markets of the Midwest, the West Coast, and even the East Coast. The railroad industry came to dominate the American transportation sector for the remainder of the nineteenth century. When Congress subsidized the first transcontinental railroad in 1862, the railroad mileage in the nation was slightly more than 30,000; by 1900 it was nearly 200,000.

As the railroad industry grew, it became apparent that competition among multiple railroad lines created inefficiencies in hauling passengers and freight for long distances. In addition, railroad corporations were incorporated in different states and were thus governed by state laws even though most of their business crossed state lines. To deal with those problems, lawyers for railroads arranged mergers among the principal railroad lines, forming large interstate railroad corporations whose assets were placed in holding companies incorporated in individual states. By 1900, two-thirds of the railroad mileage across the nation was controlled by seven such holding companies.

The emergence of transcontinental railroad networks had a major effect on the development of the nation's industrial enterprise in the late nineteenth and early twentieth centuries. By the Civil War, the mass production of goods in factories was already in place, and interstate railroads made possible the long-distance shipment of these goods. "Heavy" industries—those that developed multiple uses for natural resources such as iron ore, oil, and gas—shipped their products on railroad cars and were able to secure favorable shipping rates by virtue of the volume and frequency of their shipping. Over time, consolidation took place in the heavy industry sector as well, as lawyers facilitated mergers among competitors that resembled those in the railroad industry, resulting in the creation of giant corporations, such as U.S. Steel and Standard Oil, whose stock and other assets were placed in holding companies, typically located in states that gave them favorable tax or regulatory treatment.

The symbiotic relationship between railroads and industrial producers was important to the growth of industrial enterprise in the late nineteenth century but was not typically responsible for the initial market power of industrial enterprises. In many instances, their market dominance rested on the invention of a product or a process that had widespread practical application. Electrical contractors, such as the Edison General Electric Company and the Westinghouse Electric Company, capitalized on the invention of the incandescent light bulb and alternating current. The American Telephone and Telegraph Company's success rested on the invention of the telephone. The steel industry's emergence was derived from the invention of the Bessemer converter, which allowed large quantities of steel to be processed from crude iron.

Law mattered here as well, in two principal respects. First, the law of contracts provided the general framework through which industrial enterprises were created, launched, developed, and refined. The business of those enterprises rested on multiple contractual arrangements: among producers, distributors, and consumers of industrial products; between those who made, sold, and bought products and the transportation enterprises that shipped them; between industrial workers and their employees; among manufacturers of the component parts of products, those who assembled them and warehoused them, and those engaged in their retail sale. A network of contracts undergirded the entire industrial economy and established the legal rules that governed the successes and failures of industrial enterprise.

Those contracts also reflected the changing baselines of a market economy. In the colonial and revolutionary years, wage and price controls were common, and the idea of a "just price" for goods and services was regularly enforced by courts. As commercial credit, in the form of negotiable instruments that could be transferred to third parties, greatly expanded in the nineteenth century, equitable relations between the parties in a contract became deemphasized. *Swift v. Tyson*, the 1842 Supreme Court case in which Justice Joseph Story held that commercial transactions between citizens of different states could be governed by a "federal common law" of negotiable instruments rather than the laws of the states in which the transactions had taken place, arose out of a transaction in which a note secured by fraud had been transferred to a third party who had no notice of the circumstances of its origin and sought to enforce it against the endorser. Story concluded that "bona fide purchasers" who took such notes for consideration, and without notice of the equities between the original parties, could rely on the notes' validity. Facilitating market transactions by encouraging the free flow of negotiable instruments prevailed over the security of investors.

Second, as inventions and developments in technology became a common feature of industrial life, the market power of industries seeking to capitalize on their inventions was greatly enhanced by their ability to secure legal protection for them in the form of patents. American law had been noteworthy, from the earliest days of the republic, in granting protection to authors and inventors for their contributions. The intellectual property clause of the Constitution gave Congress the power to secure "for limited Times to Authors and Inventors the exclusive Right to their respective Writings and Discoveries." Congress responded promptly in 1790, passing statutes establishing procedures for securing patents and copyrights.

Securing a patent was comparatively easy and cheap and rested on judgments about the invention's originality rather than its marketability. Patents were typically granted for fourteen years, with the possibility of renewal, and could be assigned to others. They granted the patent-holder exclusive rights to develop, sell, and distribute the product or process and thus could be very lucrative if an invention had practical uses. The 1790 patent statute was liberally interpreted by the courts as designed to encourage invention by offering those who patented their inventions a clear advantage in securing profit from them. Thus patent law, along with mergers, acquisitions, and the creation of holding companies, contributed to both the form and scope of industrial enterprise in the late nineteenth century.

Emergence of communications media

As late as the 1920s, the leading entrepreneurial ventures in America remained those associated with the large-scale manufacture and distribution of the products of heavy industry. But as the value of offering those products to mass markets came to be perceived, industries for communicating information to mass audiences emerged. Newspapers had been present in America since the eighteenth century, but in the first decades of the twentieth century, as compulsory public education helped raise literacy levels, newspapers became ubiquitous, with each major city having several. The revenues of this industry came not only from circulation but from advertising: the advertising agency, whose job was to publicize the products of its clients in attractive ways, became a fixture of early twentieth-century business life. Newspapers and advertising agencies had a common emphasis that distinguished them from other business enterprises: the product they sold was information.

Here, once again, the development of new entrepreneurial activities was greatly facilitated by improvements in transportation and mass communication. As the railroad, the telegraph, and the telephone reduced communication distances and printing presses became more efficient, newspapers and advertisers were able to reach more customers. And in the 1920s another communications industry emerged as radio—the wireless communication of signals across space from transmitting to receiving devices—became commercialized. Initially developed by the armed forces to transmit messages in wartime or distress conditions, wireless sets were adapted to household use, and for-profit radio stations came into being.

Initially, anyone could enter the radio industry by obtaining a license from the U.S. Department of Commerce, and in the early years of the 1920s such licenses were freely given out. But two problems surfaced. One was the phenomenon of "spectrum interference" by signals of stations located close to one another on the available broadcast spectrum (the limited portion of the earth's atmosphere where sound waves could be transmitted over distances). Initially, stations that received licenses simply selected a frequency on the spectrum and began broadcasting. Because atmospheric conditions enabled signals to be heard over longer distances in the evening hours, signals from out-of-town stations could be picked up in areas where local stations were broadcasting, and when local and out-of-town frequencies had similar bandwidth, interference resulted. The federal government, which claimed jurisdiction over the airwaves, recognized that broadcast frequencies needed to be assigned.

The second problem was with the content of radio broadcasts. From the first appearance of radio, programs featured advertisements and political or religious messages. Some of the advertisements appeared to be misleading, and some of the attitudes expressed by commentators on stations were perceived as offensive by certain groups. In 1927, Congress created the Federal Radio Commission (FRC), whose powers included the assignment of frequencies and the regulation of content. In 1934, the FRC was abolished and replaced by the Federal Communications Commission (FCC), which assumed power to regulate not only radio but telephone and telegraph communications. From their outset, the FRC and the FCC were given mandates to regulate "in the public interest," which allowed them not only to dole out broadcast licenses but to review them on the basis of content. In its initial years, the FCC was strongly biased in favor of "highbrow" programming, featuring classical music concerts and public affairs programs.

The radio industry expanded greatly in the decade of the 1930s, when the number of households having radio sets increased from two in five to four in five. As that expansion took place, owners of stations grasped the efficiency of network programming, in which local stations were affiliated with nationwide networks whose programs could be developed in one place and duplicated in stations across the country. Initially, stations were grouped into two major networks, the National Broadcasting Company and the Columbia Broadcast System. (NBC had two networks, the Blue and the Red.) Since networking greatly reduced the cost of programming and the networks could combine national and local advertising on their broadcasts, the profitability of radio broadcasting soared as more households acquired sets. Another of the FCC's biases was in favor of local public affairs programs, such as news, weather, and crop reports, so local stations emerged as competitors with newspapers.

The next major innovation in communications media was television. The decade of the 1950s was to television as that of the 1920s was to radio: by 1960 more than 80 percent of American households owned a television set. Television programming initially mirrored that of radio, with the same networks that had become established in the radio industry (CBS, NBC, and the American Broadcasting Company, an offshoot of one of the NBC networks) dominating television. Once again, the FCC encouraged networks to run a combination of network shows, generated from one source, and local news and public affairs shows. The FCC distributed licenses and controlled the process by which they were renewed. Initially, the television broadcast spectrum was limited

5. The number of American households purchasing radio sets dramatically increased in the 1920s. But the legal framework for regulating the radio industry did not initially keep pace with that development. There was no regulation of the content of programming, and interference among competing broadcast signals was common.

to "very high frequency" (VHF) channels in a narrow band, which included channels 1–6 in 1941 (channel 1 was used by the armed services) and added channels 7–13 in 1945. The narrow spectrum meant that the market for television franchises was limited, so as long as broadcasting was exclusively on VHF channels, owning a television station could be very lucrative. From their origins, radio and television stations were "free" to listeners or viewers (absent the cost of acquiring a set). Operators of stations made their money from advertising.

In 1952, recognizing the growing demand for television programs and the limited number of VHF channels, the FCC authorized broadcasting on "ultra high frequency" (UHF) channels, which could send out signals on a broader spectrum and provided better reception in dense urban areas. These signals were more powerful than VHF ones but could not travel long distances. Although the FCC anticipated that the UHF market would grow exponentially and result in more diverse programming (UHF broadcasters were typically independent stations with no network affiliations), this did not occur, for two reasons. First, the signals of UHF stations were difficult to pick up outside their immediate broadcast area, and UHF stations could not rely on networks to duplicate their programs elsewhere. Second, UHF stations needed to create all their own programming, which meant that unless they achieved a niche in the television market, they would have difficulty recovering the costs of program creation. Many UHF stations turned to local sports programming, which was less costly to produce and could be directed primarily to local markets.

The result of the limited range and specialized programming of UHF stations was that few of the UHF channels allocated by the FCC were filled in most areas. Instead, proliferation of television channels and a greater diversification of television programming came from another source, initially unanticipated by the FCC. In order to improve reception in remote areas, communities began erecting antenna stations (called "head ends") in areas of high elevation and running signals from them to locations in the community by coaxial cables. The use of cables for transmission ensured that the quality of the signals would remain high, but cable operators typically needed to secure permits and easements from municipalities for running the cables. Eventually, a system of cable franchising, controlled by cities and towns, sprang up throughout the United States. Most municipalities restricted themselves to one or a very few cable franchises in order to limit the number of coaxial cables, which for most of the twentieth-century history of cable television were installed above ground.

Unlike network television, cable television was sold directly to consumers in the form of "packages" that often included large numbers of channels, both VHF and UHF. Sometimes the packages contained channels on the same network from different cities. Because cable providers typically had no or little competition in a particular area, they were able to charge what the market would bear. The FCC, however, assumed regulatory jurisdiction over cable television shortly after the industry began to surface.

The FCC's regulation of cable television brought to the surface constitutional issues that had been lurking in the background as the communications media became arguably the dominant form of American entrepreneurial activity in the middle and late twentieth century. Constitutional challenges to the FCC's regulation of content on radio and television were quite late in appearing because traditionally the broadcast media and motion pictures were placed in a different category from print media with respect to content-based regulations on expression. Whereas regulations on arguably "indecent" content in newspapers or magazines had been challenged as violating the First or Fourteenth Amendments from the 1940s on, as late as 1952 the Supreme Court had not held that the content of motion pictures was a form of protected expression. When the Court concluded that movies were a form of free speech, the Academy of Motion Pictures responded by establishing a board to rate the content of pictures, thereby giving notice of their potentially offensive content.

Meanwhile the FCC proceeded as if its mandate to regulate network broadcasting in the public interest could justify censorship of the content of programs. In a 1978 case the Court held that the FCC could fine a radio station for broadcasting a program with "indecent" content (a monologue attempting a humorous treatment of "seven dirty words") during hours when minors might be exposed to the program. Although a 1989 Court decision struck down a law passed by Congress prohibiting the interstate transmission of indecent telephone messages, the Court has not expressly held that FCC attempts to censor indecent programming on cable channels might also violate the First Amendment. Cable operators have argued that since the owners of cable packages can filter the content of the programs they select, they resemble telephone users more than radio listeners, who might unexpectedly be exposed to programs with indecent content. In 1996 and 2000 decisions, the Court seems to have agreed, invalidating efforts to require cable operators to "scramble" programs with indecent content when parental blocking devices were available.

Another First Amendment challenge arising out of the television industry came when cable operators resisted the FCC's "must carry" rules, which required them to include certain percentages of network programming in their cable packages, on the ground that the rules interfered with their editorial discretion, which was protected by the First Amendment. In two closely divided decisions handed down in 1994 and 1997, Court majorities upheld the rules as furthering an important governmental interest in preserving cable carriage of local broadcast stations. The rules were efforts to regulate the structure of the market for television programming rather than the content of broadcasts. Although the must-carry rules have been controversial within the television industry, their impact has arguably been minimal, since at present cable operators rely heavily on the programming generated by networks and might find it prohibitively expensive to create their own programs.

As cable operators were reshaping the television industry, another ubiquitous medium of communication emerged, the Internet. Like radio, computers and the Internet were initially products that were developed in the military and scientific communities and became commercialized after becoming adapted to home use through microtechnology. Once home computers became technologically feasible and their signals capable of being transmitted over "wireless" commercial satellites as well as telephone cables, the computer industry experienced massive growth, and the Internet—a global network of existing computer networks— became a source of diverse programming. From the first appearance of Internet communications, regulating the content of posts on the Internet raised special problems. The jurisdictional reach of the Internet was so broad that regulatory authority over it was uncertain; many Internet postings were anonymous; and filtering access to websites was difficult. Despite those problems, Congress attempted to protect minors from "indecent" and "patently offensive" communications on the Internet in the Communications Decency Act of 1996 and the Child Online Protection Act of 2003. The Court struck both efforts down as unduly interfering with the free speech rights of adults, signaling that it was treating Internet communications as analogous to those in the print media rather than those in the network broadcasting industry. In both cases, Court majorities referred to blocking and filtering software that parents could use to prevent children from gaining access to websites with objectionable conduct.

Thus, the twenty-first-century legal framework of the communications industry is, as the Supreme Court has put it, medium-specific. Network broadcasting remains the most regulated industry, cable television is less so, print media and the Internet are relatively free from regulation, and the motion picture industry self-regulates through its rating system. Since entrepreneurial ventures in mass communication have become the dominant form of enterprise in the late twentieth and twenty-first centuries, one can expect this framework's reach to expand in the future.

From the colonial years through the twentieth century, each of the dominant entrepreneurial ventures that emerged were responses to the changing physical and social features of the expanding American nation. Each was also made possible by legal innovations, whether in the form of a system for recording land titles, state-private partnerships creating exclusive transportation franchises, the application of patent law to inventions in the industrial sector, or the licensing of radio and television stations and cable franchises. As the main thrust of entrepreneurial activity shifted again in the twentieth century from industrial production to the marketing, communications, and entertainment sectors, aspiring entrepreneurs would continue to rely on law to facilitate their ventures, to assist them in securing market power, and to set the permissible limits of their activities.

Chapter 5
Criminal law

Criminal law in America, since its origins, has been a mix of three elements. The first element concerns the changing definitions of criminal acts, those deemed outside the realm of appropriate social conduct and thus requiring sanctions by the state. The second element concerns the policing of that criminal behavior to preserve social order and stability: the use of private and governmental institutions to keep the peace by enforcing codes of conduct and segregating criminals from society at large.

The third element of criminal law can be understood as the converse of the first two. It is the establishment of legal procedures designed to protect individuals from the unmerited exercise of criminalization or incarceration powers by officials of the state. As definitions of criminal activity have widened over the course of American history and the policing of antisocial conduct has become more common, concerns have been raised about the potential use of criminal law as a mechanism for punishing marginalized persons or groups. In response to those concerns, American criminal law has come to include a battery of constitutional procedural protections designed to curtail misuse of the power of officials to define crimes and to punish criminals.

The colonial years through the framing of the Constitution

As colonial settlements became established in America in the seventeenth century, the settlements used their origin countries' criminal law to maintain social order among both their own people and the American Indian tribes. The Indian and European responses to criminal behavior were strikingly different. Tribal societies emphasized collective responsibility for crimes; European ones emphasized individual penalties. Jurisdictional difficulties emerged when settlers and tribal members killed one another. Over time, colonial courts increasingly claimed the power to try Indians for offenses against settlers, and as European settlements were expanded, the authority of European courts over Indians increased.

During the same period, European settlements promulgated codes defining criminal offenses. In some colonies, these codes amounted to martial law, revealing the colony's concerns with fostering communal unity and suppressing social disorder in a perilous environment. In addition, most of the inhabitants of settlement communities performed forms of service labor, and laws subjected slaves and indentured servants to criminal penalties for running away or not completing their terms of service.

As the settler population of the American colonies became overwhelmingly British in the eighteenth century, settlers brought with them two features of the treatment of criminals in Great Britain. One was the public nature of punishments: numerous offenses were punished not by incarceration but by public ceremonies of whipping or branding or the display of offenders in stocks. The apogee of such punishments were public hangings, which attracted large crowds and often featured speeches decrying the offenders' conduct.

The second feature of English criminal law was the proliferation of capital crimes. By the opening of the eighteenth century almost two hundred crimes, ranging from murder to the theft of articles valued above a certain amount, could yield the death penalty. Although several alternative punishments for capital offenses existed, including deportation (called "transportation") to a British colony, and consequently few death sentences were actually carried out, the laws of the British colonies in America retained numerous capital offenses.

During the late eighteenth century, the implementation of criminal law in the American colonies became increasingly connected to the goals of colonial administration under the British Empire. As a result, when colonial Americans moved closer to independence in the 1770s, criminal law and its implementation by colonial officials became a symbol of tyrannical British rule, and local mobs or juries advanced their own interpretations of criminal conduct.

In the same time frame, some elite groups in Great Britain began to object to public punishment, believing that it glorified rather than deterred violence and that the focus of the criminal law should be on the rehabilitation of offenders. Those attitudes came to have some influence in the northern American colonies, but public punishment continued in the South, especially in states with large slave populations. Southern states were slow to move away from an emphasis on public corporal punishment even in the case of nonslave offenders.

By the time the American colonies declared their independence from Great Britain, punishment practices in southern states continued to reinforce a hierarchical labor system while having evolved in northern states away from public punishment and toward incarceration and rehabilitation. Then, with independence, protection for individuals against the arbitrary use of criminal sanctions by government officials emerged as one of the first principles of republican government. Several of the Bill of Rights amendments to the 1787 Constitution dealt with the potentially arbitrary uses of criminal law. The Fourth Amendment established protection from "unreasonable searches and seizures" by government authorities and prohibited them from issuing search warrants except on probable cause. The Fifth Amendment prohibited the trying of individuals twice for the same offense, witnessing against oneself in any criminal case, and the charging of anyone with "a capital, or otherwise infamous crime" without an indictment before a grand jury. The Sixth Amendment provided for speedy trials and trials by jury in all criminal cases and required persons accused of crimes to "be informed of the nature and cause of the accusation," to "be confronted with the witnesses against [them]," to "have compulsory process for obtaining witnesses in [their] favor," and to have the assistance of counsel in their defense. The Eighth Amendment outlawed excessive bail and excessive fines as well as "cruel and unusual punishments." Taken together, those amendments underscored the framers' conviction that the new federal republican government they were creating would not be able to use the criminal law to bully, harass, or arbitrarily imprison its citizens.

By the beginning of the nineteenth century, some distinctive features of American criminal law were in place. It would be promulgated and implemented at the state level: the federal government, which had jurisdiction over the governance of federal territories, the high seas, and the District of Columbia, was regarded as having only a limited power to create "common law" criminal offenses, and federal criminal statutes were uncommon. American criminal law would thus be diverse in its content and application, reflecting the different regional attitudes and values that emerged as the United States vastly expanded in the first half of the nineteenth century. This meant that different theories of punishment and uses of the prison system came to coexist. Some states emphasized the incarcerative and disciplinary dimensions of the system, building "escape proof" prisons and severely restricting the privileges of inmates. Others stressed rehabilitation, encouraging prisoners to learn tasks and rewarding them for cooperative behavior.

In addition, the constitutional protections afforded criminal defendants by the Bill of Rights demonstrated that many Americans associated the idea of individual rights with freedom from the arbitrary or excessive use of criminal sanctions by the state and its officials. The principle that government officials needed to respect the "rights" of persons coming in contact with the criminal process would become one of the linchpins of American constitutional jurisprudence.

One defining element in American criminal law had not yet emerged by the opening of the nineteenth century: the idea that localities, states, and eventually the federal government should supply professional police forces to enforce criminal laws and protect the public from criminal behavior. Eventually, members of police forces would emerge as the primary enforcers of the criminal law, but for much of the nineteenth century those forces were nonexistent. Instead, private citizens would be summoned to respond to antisocial behavior, as when a "hue and cry" would go up when someone had been accused of theft or an assault against a citizen. White citizen "slave patrols" investigated the status of African Americans traveling without masters to see if they were enslaved and attempting to escape.

Criminal law, policing, and punishment in the nineteenth century

Over the course of the nineteenth century, the nation more than doubled in size, witnessed significant immigration and population growth, experienced a civil war and the abolition of slavery, and underwent an economic transformation, with industrial capitalism making considerable incursions on agricultural householding as the dominant form of economic activity. These changes would have noticeable effects on each of the central elements of criminal law.

As northern states retreated from an emphasis on public corporal punishments, they also reduced the number of capital crimes and placed a greater emphasis on the rehabilitation of offenders. Over the first three decades of the nineteenth century, the legislatures of Massachusetts, New York, and Pennsylvania established "degrees" of murder and manslaughter, reserving capital punishment only for first degree murder, and by the 1850s the number of capital offenses in southern as well as northern states had been significantly reduced. The decline of public corporal punishment meant, however, that more criminals were incarcerated for lengthy periods, and the institution of the penitentiary evolved out of that development.

Penitentiaries embodied two theories of criminal punishment. One was that physical violence and public shaming were less effective responses to criminal behavior than forcibly separating offenders from society. The other was that the state could profit from the compulsory labor of prison residents. After building prisons, states sought to take advantage of the labor inmates could provide. Throughout the nineteenth century, several states expanded the range of work for inmates and entered into arrangements to profit from their labor. Those arrangements included leasing the work of inmates to private contractors, such as shoemakers, manufacturers of farm equipment, and furniture distributors, who marketed the resulting products. The buildings where prisoners were housed were also leased to private businesses, and one state, Missouri, leased inmates to perform domestic services in private households.

As sectors of the industrial labor force became unionized in the nineteenth century, unions in some states objected to competing against prison labor and at times succeeded in getting state legislatures to ban prison labor in certain industries. Even today, though, states continue to lease prisoners to the private sector. Meanwhile, "chain gang" prisoner labor continues to be employed on many state public works projects. The building of prisons in the nineteenth century was a reflection of altered theories of punishment rather than a response to increased crime. But with the massive growth of the American urban population in that century, concerns about crime and social disorder in cities increased, and professional urban police forces emerged.

The early history of municipal police forces in America suggests a direct correlation between their creation and public fears of social unrest. During the eighteenth and early nineteenth centuries, threats to the public peace in communities were met by volunteer groups of citizens, supplemented on occasion by members of local or state militias. Those forces were not standing operations; they were organized in response to discrete incidents. Communities typically had sheriffs and constables, who administered the treatment of crimes and criminals, but did not engage in general policing. The assumption behind those practices was that criminal activity was not the norm and when it surfaced citizens could readily be summoned to respond.

There were, however, places where community forces engaged in general policing: southern cities with large slave populations. The "slave patrols," which were first formed in Charleston, South Carolina, in the late seventeenth century, subsequently evolved into standing police forces. By the opening of the nineteenth century, both Charleston and New Orleans, the two most populous cities in the slaveholding south, had police departments. In both cities, members of the police were paid, armed, and uniformed along military lines. The principal task of the police was to enforce municipalities' and states' requirements that African Americans carry "pass papers" within their borders. These papers, which identified the bearer by name and the purpose of his or her journey, were designed to discourage slaves from running away, distinguish slaves from free blacks, and make it easier to obtain evidence about potential slave insurrections. By the Civil War, almost all southern cities had police forces.

By the 1840s, police forces had also begun to emerge in larger northern cities, such as Boston, New York, and Philadelphia, responding to a threat affluent residents of those cities saw as analogous to potential slave revolts: urban riots by immigrants. During the 1830s and 1840s, as large numbers of European immigrants settled in northern coastal cities and joined a growing class of wage laborers, ethnic and religious tensions surfaced as gangs of immigrant laborers competed for jobs. When riots involving immigrant and native laborers broke out, affluent residents of cities feared for the safety of their property and themselves, leading to the creation of police forces.

By the Civil War, Boston, New York, Philadelphia, and Chicago had municipal police forces organized on a military model, but the older tradition of voluntary, "extralegal" responses to sporadic outbreaks of crime or social disorder persisted. Nineteenth-century extralegal responses to antisocial behavior can be grouped into two categories. One category was composed of responses sanctioned by the norms of honor culture, such as responses to attacks or slights on an individual's name or family reputation. Such actions were regarded as justifying violent public responses, such as fights, whippings, and duels, from males defending their own or their families' honor. From the late eighteenth century through the Civil War, dueling, although typically illegal, was rarely prosecuted, even when a participant was killed. Other killings motivated by affronts to the perpetrator's honor, such as the seduction of his wife by another man, were often either excused or given reduced penalties.

The other category of extralegal response was vigilante justice, which took several forms. Some responses consisted of social ostracism, such as expulsion from church congregations or banishment from the community. Others involved mob violence directed at groups or individuals, including the lynching of persons suspected of committing crimes that were thought particularly heinous. The ultimate example was the reaction to perceived sexual assaults by African Americans on white women and children. Nearly four thousand African American males, many of whom had been charged with sexual assaults, were lynched between the 1880s and the 1930s.

The twentieth century

In the first two decades of the twentieth century, the federal government became more involved in the enforcement of criminal law. One reason for its increased presence was an altered attitude toward the causes of crime and the treatment of criminals. Rehabilitative theories of punishment became dominant as scholarship in the social sciences suggested that the causes of criminal activity were societal and could be identified and remedied, and commissions were created to make national recommendations. These studies revealed that local police forces regularly resorted to physical abuse to secure convictions and the decisions of law enforcement officials were regularly influenced by politics. Academics called for the imposition of national standards of criminal procedure.

Two other early twentieth-century developments increased the federal government's involvement in law enforcement. One was the emergence, in the wake of World War I, of federal legislation directed at "subversive" activity. Although statutes such as the Sedition and Espionage Acts of 1917 were products of the war, they remained in place after its end. In response to the Red Scare of 1919 and 1920, brought about by fears that newly arrived immigrants from Europe had brought collectivist ideologies with them, the Justice Department made an effort to identify, detain, and deport suspected subversives. That department's Bureau of Investigation (subsequently known as the FBI) spearheaded the effort, and in the 1930s the FBI significantly expanded its presence and transferred its attention to domestic organized crime. States also responded to the Red Scare by passing legislation outlawing various collectivist ideologies, such as syndicalism, anarchism, and communism, and constitutional challenges to this legislation were advanced.

Between 1900 and 1916, twenty-one states, responding to a wave of prohibitionist sentiment, banned saloons, and others sought to restrict the sale of alcoholic beverages. The prohibition movement eventually resulted in the Eighteenth Amendment to the Constitution (1919) and its implementing federal legislation, the Volstead Act. These two measures outlawed the manufacture, sale, or interstate transportation of beverages that contained more than 0.5 percent alcohol and established the federal Bureau of Internal Revenue as enforcement agent. An unanticipated consequence of national prohibition was the emergence of organized crime. Although prohibition served to reduce the public consumption of alcohol throughout the 1920s, it also created a thriving bootleg market for the manufacture and interstate transportation of alcoholic beverages. When the Eighteenth Amendment closed down establishments associated with the liquor business, those entrepreneurs turned to illicit operations. The organized crime syndicates that emerged in the nation's large cities in the 1920s were initially centered on the liquor trade. They formed associations with politicians and transportation companies and soon controlled the manufacture, sale, and transportation of bootleg liquor.

The Volstead Act made the distribution of alcoholic beverages across state lines a federal crime. Since bootleggers typically received higher profits from the interstate transportation of alcoholic beverages, it increased significantly, and so did the law enforcement apparatus of the federal government. By 1930, more than a third of the inmates in the nation's federal prison system were persons convicted of violating the Volstead Act. That statistic demonstrates that a major effect of prohibition was the growth of federal prisons. As late as the 1890s, the federal government had no prisons at all; the small number of persons jailed for committing federal crimes were held in state prisons. State prisons became less profitable in the early twentieth century after organized labor opposed their efforts to hire out inmates or sell products made by them, and Congress began to experiment with some federal prisons. By the 1930s only seven existed, but the enforcement of the Volstead Act meant that they held more than twelve thousand inmates.

As the visibility of organized crime increased during the late 1920s and 1930s and the federal government became more involved in domestic crime fighting, a reconsideration of the basis of crime emerged. Studies of local and state criminal justice systems commissioned by the federal government had revealed two underemphasized features of twentieth-century criminal law and its administration. First, criminal justice was highly dependent on prosecutorial and judicial discretion, with much of its administration consisting of decisions to prosecute or to enter into plea bargains. Second, local and state law enforcement practices in many jurisdictions were often brutal and sometimes flagrantly illegal, with the police regularly securing involuntary confessions by means of physical abuse.

The surveys exposed the fact that in the 1930s, most persons accused of crimes were not afforded any uniform constitutional safeguards. This was because none of the protections afforded criminal defendants in the Bill of Rights were treated as applying to the states. State law enforcement officials could operate without having to comply with provisions prohibiting unreasonable searches and seizures, compulsory self-incrimination, and cruel and unusual punishments and requiring persons charged with crimes to be represented by attorneys. The level of legal protection for criminally accused persons in a state was only as high as state officials chose to make it, and in some instances, as when African Americans were charged with crimes in southern states, that meant virtually no protection at all.

By the 1950s, however, the procedural dimensions of criminal justice were on their way to being transformed, as the U.S. Supreme Court began to apply a series of Bill of Rights protections for criminal defendants against the states. When Earl Warren, a former California prosecutor, became chief justice in 1953, a majority of the Court was poised to apply most of the Bill of Rights provisions for these safeguards. By the time Warren retired in 1969, the Fourth Amendment's protection against unreasonable searches and seizures, the Fifth Amendment's self-incrimination and double jeopardy provisions, and the Sixth Amendment's guarantee of trial by jury had been applied against the states through the Fourteenth Amendment's due process clause. Most visible of all the Court's criminal procedure rulings were those providing that persons taken into custody by state or local police were entitled to legal representation and, once detained, must be advised that they could remain silent during interrogation. Taken together, the Court's criminal procedure decisions transformed state law enforcement regimes with broad official discretion into agencies subjected to significant legal oversight.

In the latter half of the twentieth century, when this constitutionalization of American criminal law occurred, elite public opinion still largely endorsed environmental theories of the causes of crime and rehabilitative theories of punishment. By the late 1960s, it was clear that many other segments of American society did not share that view. A perception that increased protection for criminal defendants had intensified crime fueled a growing "law and order" mentality among candidates for public office, who charged that permissive judges were turning criminals loose on the streets on the basis of "legal technicalities."

Beginning in the 1980s, successive presidents launched "wars" on crime, whose principal effect was to greatly increase the American prison population, which was disproportionately made up of African-American males. In 1980, slightly more than 500,000 persons were prison inmates; in 1990 the number had increased to 1.5 million; by 2000 it was nearly 2 million. The prison population continued to increase despite the fact that the rate of major crimes dropped significantly in the last decade of the twentieth century. Perhaps the most striking statistic about the crime population involved the incarceration of nonviolent offenders. In 2000, the number of drug offenders in prison was thirteen times that in 1980, and in the same time span the number of "public order" offenders (those engaged in nonviolent moral offenses) increased from 12,400 to 124,600. In contrast, the number of violent offenders in 2000 was only three times that in 1980.

The data revealed that the swelling of the American prison population had come primarily from the imposition of longer sentences for nonviolent offenses and that retributive models of punishment were back in fashion. A boom in prison building took place in the last decades of the twentieth century, emphasizing high-security institutions, some managed by private companies.

Thus, American criminal law entered the twenty-first century in what might appear, from the perspective of history, a somewhat paradoxical state. The historically regional and diverse character of criminal law and its administration was decisively altered in the twentieth century as the federal government became a major

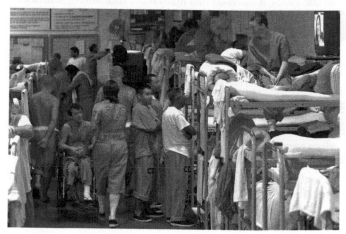

6. This photo of overcrowding in a California prison was appended to the opinion of the Supreme Court in *Brown v. Plata*, 131 S.Ct. 1910 (2011), in which a majority of the Court held that a limit on the prison population of the state was required in order to protect prisoners' right to be free from "cruel and unusual punishment" under the Eighth Amendment to the U.S. Constitution.

presence in law enforcement and the Supreme Court imposed uniform constitutional requirements on state law enforcement officials. As American criminal law became constitutionalized, convictions became more difficult to obtain, and a perception surfaced that crime was increasing as offenders escaped conviction. That attitude resulted in policy-makers imposing longer fixed sentences and imprisoning more nonviolent offenders, particularly drug users. The result, since the 1980s, has been a decrease in major crimes but a massive swelling of the prison population, with less attention being directed toward the rehabilitation of its members.

Crime and the treatment of criminals have been pervasive and perplexing themes of American legal history. In contrast to the early conceptions of crime and punishment as largely private activities, diagnosing and responding to crime has become a distinctly public activity, as susceptible to changing public attitudes as any other sector of American political life. On the one hand, Americans have been responsive to the idea that individual citizens have rights not to be subjected to arbitrary criminal process by the state; on the other they have rarely been opposed to the prospect of criminals being locked up for a long time. Balancing those attitudes has not been easy, and at present the balance seems tipped toward incarceration. The United States leads the world in the percentage of its inhabitants who are in prison.

Chapter 6
Law and domestic relations

Few areas of American legal history have changed so dramatically over the course of time, or shown so close a concordance with shifting public attitudes, as the law of domestic relations, which governs marriage, divorce, and the treatment of children. In the years between American independence and the outset of the twenty-first century, domestic relations law in the United States has undergone two noticeable transformations. First, the legal rules of domestic relations came to be separated from those of masters and servants in a newly conceived "domestic" sphere, sharply distinguished from the occupational spheres of life. Second, the domestic realm, while continuing to be understood as a private sanctuary from the outside world, has increasingly come to be shaped, maintained, and policed by officials of the state.

The extended household of early America

At approximately the same time that the British colonies in America were setting themselves on a path of separation from the British Empire, William Blackstone published the first edition of *Commentaries on the Law of England*, which became the most influential legal treatise in late eighteenth- and early nineteenth-century America. In a description of "the law of persons" in his *Commentaries*, he summarized what he took to be the predominant character of households and their members. He understood a "household" as an economic as well as a social unit, composed of a male head, wives and children, indentured and other servants, wage-earning laborers, apprentices, wards (persons for whom a guardian had formal legal responsibility), and slaves. All of the members performed tasks associated with their roles, and all were in a dependent relationship with the head. The relationship of a husband and his wife was treated as analogous to that of a father and his children, a master and his servant, or a guardian and his ward. In households, the legal powers and identities of wives, children, servants, and wards were subordinate to those of the head and were derived from the degree and nature of the protection the head provided them.

Blackstone's characterization treated marriage, parenting, guardianship, and the employment of servants as part of an extended domain of householding characterized by hierarchical human relationships, versions of the relationship between master and servant. His description of the legally dependent status of wives, children, and servants was not an accurate rendering of law and practice in seventeenth- and eighteenth-century England and colonial America. Nonetheless, his starting premise—that women and children were categories of dependent beings, analogous to wards and servants—was retained by Tapping Reeve, who published the first American legal treatise on household relationships in 1816. In describing those relationships, Reeve employed Blackstone's categories and emphasized the themes of legal control and protection, and legal subordination and dependency, associated with domestic life.

By the time Reeve's treatise appeared, changes had begun to affect the roles of members of households in colonial and revolutionary America. Although slaves remained in a position of legal, social, and economic dependency on those who owned them, other household workers were increasingly able to cast off their dependent status. As the tenures of male indentured servants and apprentices expired, most of them were able to use their training to become independent wage earners in an economy dominated by agricultural householding, earning income from their labor skills, acquiring land, and eventually establishing their own households. The United States' purchase of large amounts of territory from France and Spain in the first two decades of the nineteenth century helped male former household workers become wage earners and eventually freeholders. The cumulative effect of these changes was to significantly increase the number of male workers who were not members of households, either in the sense that their jobs were connected to a single householding enterprise or that the terms of their labor were modeled on the relationship of masters and servants.

One might have thought that as more male Americans engaged in jobs that did not involve some version of a master-servant relationship, the resulting economic and social independence for so many men might have radiated through all the members of nonslaveholding households. Instead, the withdrawal of male indentured servants and apprentices from households created a "domestic" sphere of householding, in which the status of male heads of households was differentiated from that of women and younger children. Thus, even though some developments in the early nineteenth century, such as the legislative extensions of suffrage beyond freeholders, promoted the independence and autonomy of individuals, Blackstone's conceptions of married women as having no legal identity independent of their husbands and of fathers retaining primary authority over their children remained in place throughout the first half of the century.

The emergence of the "domestic" household

By the middle of the nineteenth century, many American households no longer contained multiple versions of master-servant relationships. Nonetheless, not all members of a household were commonly accepted as autonomous individuals. Most states had enacted married women's property acts that allowed married women to buy and sell property without their husbands' consent being required. However, wives and children increasingly came to be pictured as occupants of a "domestic" realm that was separated from the largely male working world. Wives and children continued to be treated as dependent beings with respect to their husbands and fathers, but their dependency was now framed as an aspect of the stabilizing qualities of the newly conceived domestic realm, which was envisioned as protecting the integrity of the new nuclear family, the nurturing qualities of wives and mothers, the opportunities for children to remain innocent and uncorrupted, and domestic life as a sanctuary from the working world.

The decision by early nineteenth-century Americans to treat the domestic dimensions of family life as sources of stability and refinement can be seen in legal commentary from the period. By the 1820s, James Kent, in his *Commentaries on American Law*, was attributing to the institution of marriage a "great share of the blessings which flow from the refinement of manners, the education of children, the sense of justice, and the cultivation of the liberal arts." In Kent's characterization, domesticity was associated with a range of virtues, and married women were implicitly recognized as agents who performed a variety of socially valuable tasks. Children as well were no longer seen as a species of miniature adults performing apprentice roles but as "tender" beings open to moral and social education as well as more traditional learning.

The carving out of a domestic sphere of life and the association of that sphere with the virtues of stability, refinement, and the moral education of children transformed the household from its earlier role as an institution primarily designed for the procreation of legitimate children, the orderly transfer of property, and the demarcation of roles paralleling those of masters and servants. The household came to be viewed as a setting where the gendered occupational and domestic spheres of life complemented one other, lending strength and stability to nuclear family units. Over the course of the nineteenth century, this transformation of the conception of American households had several effects on what came to be known as domestic relations law.

First, a recognition of the domestic virtues associated with marriage resulted in an elevation of the status of being married. In England, and initially in America, formal sanctioning of a marriage by the state was required. But by the second decade of the nineteenth century American couples were increasingly entering into "common law" marriages, where couples simply lived together in the fashion of husband and wife and states tacitly acknowledged the arrangement.

Second, divorce, which was inconsistent with the traditional view that the legal identity of husband and wife were one, was implemented by most American states after independence. "Fault" was a required ground for divorce, and adultery, desertion, and cruelty were the primary bases for fault. The early American recognition of divorce suggests that a conception of marriage as fostering "domestic" virtues was beginning to emerge by the last decades of the eighteenth century. If the primary purposes of marriage were procreation and the orderly transfer of property within families, divorce might have the effect of undermining those goals. But if marriage was also a mechanism for promoting values such as the integrity of the nuclear family, refinement in manners and morals, and attentiveness to the education of children, then adultery, cruelty, or desertion were inconsistent with those expectations. By engaging in those practices, participants in a marriage were signaling that they no longer subscribed to the companionable dimensions of domesticity. They were thus "at fault," and their spouses could sever relations with them.

Although the increase in divorce and the emergence of common law marriages can be seen as originating from similar premises about the institution of marriage, they evolved in a strikingly different fashion in nineteenth-century America. Because the status of marriage was regarded as socially desirable, private behavior signaling that two persons had a common law marriage was simply ratified, not evaluated, by state officials. In contrast, state judges decided whether to grant divorces, and jurisdictions varied widely in what they regarded as appropriate "fault" grounds. This meant that states with judicially applied divorce statutes were implicitly defining the qualities they deemed desirable and undesirable in a marriage.

The different approaches of state officials to common law marriage and divorce revealed that by the nineteenth century, the domestic character of American households had come to be treated as socially valuable and thus a matter of public concern. In allowing common law marriage, the state was tacitly sanctioning the decisions of men and women who had chosen to live together because stable, long-term relationships among males and females had come to be associated with a set of domestic virtues. With that association in place, state officials took it upon themselves to preserve the ideal of domesticity by fixing the terms under which marriages could be dissolved. Private actors were thus largely free to enter into marriage but far less free to exit it. Marriage, divorce, and child-rearing had become public concerns because of the societal benefits associated with a private domestic sphere of life.

Divorce was not the only dimension of nineteenth-century domestic relations law that illustrates states' concerns with carving out, and preserving, a sphere of life associated with companionable domestic virtues. One can see similar trends in the treatment of children, specifically in attitudes toward child custody, the status of illegitimate children, and adoption.

In the traditional Anglo-American view of family relations, the relationship of fathers and their children was analogized to that of masters and servants. Fathers were regarded as having an obligation to support their children and were expected to benefit from their children's labor. That conception of parent-child relations, when coupled with the equation of married women's legal identities with those of their husbands, resulted in "custody" of children being attached to fathers. But as the domestic sphere of household life began to be emphasized in the nineteenth century, the roles of wives and children in households came to be described differently. Wives came to be seen as the primary agents charged with fostering domestic virtues and children as innocent, vulnerable beings for whom domestic life was a process of moral development as well as occupational training. It followed from this altered conception of the roles of family members that children in a household required nurturing, a way of inculcating the values of companionability and mutual affection within a nuclear family; that women were best suited to perform nurturing functions; and that children in a household could be seen as having an expectation of being exposed to a safe, affectionate, morally instructive household environment.

Three nineteenth-century developments in the law affecting children were consistent with this altered understanding of the role of children in households. One was the altered posture of courts in custody disputes. Over the course of the century, the presumption that fathers would retain common law rights to the labor of their children should husbands and wives separate or divorce was replaced by a judicially administered "best interest of the child" standard. That standard included a "tender years" presumption that most young children were better off in the custody of their mothers.

Another development involved the treatment of illegitimacy. The traditional view of children born outside wedlock was that they were "bastards" who had no legal connections to their fathers and thus could not inherit property. Treating illegitimate children as nonpersons was consistent with legitimizing the reputation of a family and encouraging the transfer of the family's name and property from generation to generation by ensuring that only "family" members could inherit. But the widespread recognition of common law marriage in America and the association of mothers with the teaching of domestic virtues resulted in more children being accorded legitimate status, the mothers of illegitimate children being given custody of them, and illegitimate children being made eligible to share in their mothers' estates. Although those changes were designed to create incentives for mothers to maintain nurturing relationships with illegitimate as well as legitimate children, they presupposed a continuing obligation of putative fathers to provide support for children born out of wedlock. When that support was not forthcoming and was unavailable from mothers or their relatives, state officials sought to place illegitimate children with other families.

A third change involved adoption, which did not formally exist in the traditional Anglo-American law of family relations because it was inconsistent with the assumption that by legally sanctioning marriage and conferring legitimacy on children born within sanctioned families, the common law was preserving the property and reputations of persons whose generations were joined by blood ties. From that perspective, adoption diluted the integrity of families. In nineteenth-century America, however, adoption also served to bring more persons within the domestic sphere of nuclear families, thereby potentially ensuring that more children would be appropriately nurtured and educated. Beginning in the 1850s, most American states established formal adoption procedures in which adoptive parents took on the responsibilities of biological parents and adopted children were made eligible to inherit property. As with custody and illegitimacy, adoption proceedings were administered by the judiciary. A result of those modifications of traditional Anglo-American law was the extension of the power of states to define the contours of American domestic life.

Cumulatively, the changes in marriage, divorce, child custody, the treatment of illegitimacy, and adoption that took place in the first half of the nineteenth century meant that the domestic sphere was increasingly policed by state officials, most notably judges, who decided, in effect, who was to be eligible to join and who would be cast off from nuclear families. After the Civil War, this policing continued, revealing that the interest among public officials in preserving domestic households had come to be associated with "approved" forms of married life and sexual activity.

Refining the definitions of "domestic" activity

In the early nineteenth century, as state officials altered the traditional definitions of households and the roles of male heads, wives, and children in the domestic sphere of life, the control these officials assumed over American nuclear families operated exclusively at the state level. This meant that although state judges had the ability to shape the contours of domestic family life within their jurisdictions, regional rules and practices varied. Thus South Carolina could impose an absolute prohibition on divorce, whereas Indiana could serve as a place where out-of-state residents could quickly and cheaply dissolve their marriages.

Two developments connected to the Civil War resulted in the federal government assuming limited control over domestic relations law as well. The first was the increased presence of federal officials as implementers of the Thirteenth and Fourteenth Amendments, which abolished slavery and made free persons of African American descent citizens of the United States. In the course of helping former slaves become landowners and wage earners, the Freedmen's Bureau, the federal agency entrusted with those tasks, also sought to transform slave unions into marriages that states could legalize. That required a list of "marriage rules" establishing procedures by which former slaves in unions could present them for state approval. Most striking among those "rules" were prohibitions on interracial marriage, which were also routinely imposed by states in the late nineteenth century.

The federal government also regulated marriage in federal territories. After the Civil War, Utah remained a federal territory:

it did not enter the Union until 1896. Utah Territory had a number of residents who were members of the Church of Jesus Christ of Latter-day Saints, whose doctrines encouraged polygamous marriages. In its role as supervisor of the territory, the federal government claimed the power to regulate marriage within it, and in 1879 the U.S. Supreme Court held that the United States could ban polygamy in the territory, despite the fact that domestic relations law had typically been regarded as the province of the states. The American domestic household of the late nineteenth century, the Court concluded, was to be monogamous.

The domestic household was also to be one in which the sexual activity of its members was firmly associated with reproduction. Prior to the Civil War, the practice of abortion had been tacitly recognized: few states criminalized it, and those that did relied on a common law rule limiting illegal abortions to those undertaken after there had been visible movement ("quickening") of a fetus. After the war ended, vocal critics of divorce claimed that an increase in the divorce rate had led to a decline in the number of children born to nuclear families, and that both trends were symptoms of a decline in American morals. They urged Congress to pass a uniform statute restricting divorce, and although that statute failed to materialize, a congressional survey on marriage and divorce confirmed that Americans were divorcing more and having fewer children. Birth control practices were seen as consistent with those trends, since the absence of children allegedly made it easier for married couples to divorce. In 1873, Congress passed a statute criminalizing the dissemination through the mail of "obscene, lewd, or lascivious" materials, which included information about birth control devices and practices. In the next two decades, the number of states criminalizing abortion dramatically increased.

Thus, by the close of the nineteenth century the idea that the domestic sphere of households represented a sanctuary where the affectionate nurturing of children and moral education could flourish had been retained, but at the same time states and the federal government had particularized their definitions of domesticity. The forms of marriage consistent with the ideal of domesticity were those embodied in permanent, nuclear, procreative unions composed of members of the same race. Alternatives to that conception of marriage, ranging from polygamy to interracial unions to efforts on the part of married couples to restrict their childbearing, were disfavored and in some instances legally prohibited. By the close of the century, states and the federal government had replaced the older paternalism of the master-servant household regime with another species of paternalism, which equated domesticity with a set of legal rules designed to ensure that households would take some forms and not others.

Domesticity and household membership in the twentieth century

The predominant theme of twentieth-century developments in domestic relations law was a tendency to remove restrictions on the conduct of individuals in households. Over the course of the century divorce became progressively easier to obtain, first through the proliferation of jurisdictions expanding the criteria that made persons eligible for divorce, then by abandoning the once-central "fault" criterion. By the close of the century, "no-fault" divorces were available in the majority of American states. In addition, adoption requirements continued to be liberalized, the custody of children was awarded to surrogate as well as biological parents, persons "cohabitating" with others were sometimes treated comparably to married persons in property or divorce settlements, and the number of common law marriages declined because the requirements for obtaining a state-sanctioned marriage diminished.

The relaxation of official constraints on the actions of individuals in domestic relationships was also illustrated by a set of decisions

7. Couples line up to get New York marriage licenses, for a fee of
$1.00, in the early 1920s. For most of the twentieth century, the
policies of states encouraged marriage of heterosexual couples,
discouraged divorce, and outlawed same-sex unions.

by the U.S. Supreme Court. In *Griswold v. Connecticut* (1965),
Loving v. Virginia (1967), *Eisenstadt v. Baird* (1972), and *Roe v.
Wade* (1973), the Court held that neither states nor the federal
government could constitutionally prevent the distribution of birth
control information to married couples or individuals, prohibit
interracial marriage, or impose complete bans on the choice of
a woman to terminate a pregnancy. The decisions retained a
conception of domestic life as a sanctuary from the outside world
but linked that conception to the sword of individual autonomy, as
well as the shield of privacy.

But despite those trends, twentieth-century domestic relations
law cannot fully be characterized as progressively abandoning the
role of state actors as trustees of the individuals within a domestic
relationship. In approximately the same time frame in which
developments in domestic relations law expanded the autonomy of
individuals within domestic circles, Congress and the states passed
a series of laws that had the cumulative effect of encouraging

some sorts of domestic arrangements and discouraging others. One set of laws created incentives for single heterosexual males and females to marry; the other stigmatized homosexuality by criminalizing consensual sexual activity by members of the same sex and declining to treat same-sex domestic partnerships as legitimate.

From the 1930s through most of the remainder of the century, married persons, especially married women, received higher wages in the military services and other branches of federal employment, and greater benefits in the administration of Social Security and other federal and state benefit plans, than single heterosexual persons. In the same time period, homosexuality was treated as a basis for discharging persons from positions in the military or civilian governmental offices, deporting aliens, withholding veterans benefits, and dismissing teachers from public schools. The principal federal domestic law enforcement agency of the mid-twentieth century, the FBI, shifted its attention from identifying and prosecuting "morals" offenses engaged in by heterosexuals, such as prostitution or sexual liaisons with minors, to identifying persons labeled as sexual psychopaths and the dangers they posed to children.

The policing of homosexuality by federal agencies was reinforced by state laws criminalizing consensual sexual conduct among members of the same sex and preventing homosexual couples from marrying or adopting children. In *Bowers v. Hardwick* (1986), the Supreme Court of the United States sustained the constitutionality of the first set of those laws, assuming that the rights of adults to choose their domestic partners or to make decisions about their intimate relationships without state interference did not apply to homosexuals.

Taken together, those twentieth-century laws and policies demonstrated that state actors, in the role of trustees, were continuing to shape the contours of American domestic life.

Although courts and legislatures no longer prevented domestic households from being interracial, or restricted the reproductive choices of members of those households, they continued to encourage single heterosexual persons to marry and to discourage homosexuals from entering into intimate relationships. It was not until the twenty-first century that the long-standing assumption that American domestic households could legitimately be composed only of persons with heterosexual preferences was successfully challenged. In *Lawrence v. Texas* (2003), the Supreme Court overruled *Bowers v. Hardwick*, holding that states could not constitutionally criminalize consensual intimate behavior among same-sex adults. That decision has encouraged some states to legalize same-sex marriage, although other states have declined to do so, and in the Defense of Marriage Act (1996), the federal government defined marriage, for the purpose of securing federal benefits, as the union of a man and a woman. The constitutionality of the Defense of Marriage Act was invalidated by the Supreme Court in its 2012 Term.

In early America, as extended households composed of persons in several versions of master-servant relationships began to dissolve, the idea of the household as a domestic realm emerged. Paradoxically, however, the creation of a domestic sphere that would serve as a private sanctuary from the outside world stimulated the emergence of legal trustees of the state—legislatures and judges—who served to define the parameters of the domestic realm in accordance with mainstream public values. American domestic relations law thus became, and has remained, a set of public regulations for an area of life whose preservation has been deemed especially valuable because of its private character.

Chapter 7
Civil injuries and the law of torts

A systematic body of law governing the treatment of a large class of injuries to persons or property was late to develop in America. Those injuries came to be called torts—civil injuries not arising out of contractual relationships—and encompassed a broad and diverse group of actions, ranging from assaults to false statements damaging the reputations of others to accidents in workplaces or on the highways. Tort law currently governs most personal injury lawsuits, some of which occasionally result in considerable damage judgments. Contemporary tort law is also significantly affected by the presence of liability insurance. None of those characteristics of current tort law were part of its early history in America; in fact tort law was not thought of as a discrete common law field until after the Civil War.

The Anglo-American heritage

Actions that caused injury and resulted in damage but were not deemed sufficiently serious to merit criminal penalties were part of the British legal system from ancient times. The most common examples were unauthorized entry onto someone else's property (trespass), engaging in activities that caused unhealthy or offensive emissions (nuisance), putting others in reasonable fear for their safety (assault), touching others in a rude and damaging fashion (battery), and making false oral or written statements about others that were capable of damaging the others' reputations (slander or libel). Although some trespasses, nuisances, assaults, batteries, and defamations were deemed sufficiently serious to invoke criminal penalties, in many instances injured parties sought redress exclusively through private civil lawsuits, seeking compensatory and sometimes punitive damages. The injuries they complained of were known as torts.

Until the middle of the nineteenth century, the American legal profession defined civil suits that sought remedies for tortious conduct not as a separate field of law but as illustrations of the use of certain common law writs—the name for the formal civil action employed by the party seeking damages. Trespass, trespass on the case (employed for unintentional or "indirect" intrusions onto another's land), trover (employed when someone's property was intentionally or carelessly converted), nuisance, slander, libel, and fraud were types of writs. To be successfully employed, each writ needed to meet certain technical requirements, such as proving that an injury had been "direct" or "indirect," or that an allegedly noxious activity had been "continuous," or that a damaging statement about another had been "false." Use of the wrong writ or failure to meet a writ's requirements resulted in dismissal of the civil suit. So long as the crucial element in bringing a suit alleging tortious conduct was the ability to choose the correct writ and to meet its requirements, English and American courts and commentators assumed that cases involving civil injuries not arising out of contract were best understood as illustrations of the law of evidence, not as belonging to a discrete substantive field.

The emergence of torts as a common law field

In the United States between 1850 and 1880, tort actions gradually ceased to be treated as part of the law of evidence and emerged as the basis of an additional field of common law. The reasons for that development were multiple and interconnected. As the American population grew and more states joined the Union, the dockets of state courts expanded, while barriers to entry in the legal profession remained low, resulting in many people practicing law who did not have extensive technical training. Mastery of the requirements of common law writ pleading eluded many lawyers, and courts found it convenient to allow litigators to amend the form of their writs rather than to dismiss lawsuits. As the technical requirements of the writs were less strictly enforced, the writs ceased to become the equivalent of legal rules. Groups within the legal profession urged reform of the rigors of writ pleading, and by the close of the nineteenth century a general civil action, requiring proof of injury, damages, a violation of a standard of civil liability, and the showing of a causal relationship between the violation and the injury, was in place in almost all state jurisdictions.

The replacement of the writ system with a general civil action was not simply a recognition of the inability of existing writs to serve as the equivalent of rules for tort cases. The development was also based on a growing recognition that the various civil actions for injuries had something in common and could be governed by generalized standards of civil liability.

An 1850 Massachusetts case, *Brown v. Kendall*, is often cited as an illustration of the beginnings of the transformation from the writ system to general standards of civil liability. In seeking to determine the accountability of a dog owner who, in the course of using a stick to break up a dogfight, injured a person in the vicinity, the chief justice of Massachusetts, Lemuel Shaw, noted that such cases often raised "the long-vexed question, under the rule of the common law, whether a party's remedy . . . should be sought in an action of the case, or in trespass." Shaw concluded, however, that the requirements for using one writ or another were "no authority" in themselves for determining whether damage could be recovered. Liability should turn on "whether the act was "wilful, intentional, or careless."

Shaw's language suggests that he was displacing the writ system with standards of liability—"wilful, intentional, or careless"—as the basis for recovery in civil actions arising out of accidents, and many commentators have taken that language as transformative. But later in the opinion, Shaw added: "We think, as the result of all the authorities, the rule is correctly stated by Mr. Greenleaf, that the plaintiff must come prepared with evidence to show either that the *intention* was unlawful, or that the defendant was *in fault.*" Shaw's reference to "Mr. Greenleaf"—Simon Greenleaf, the author of a treatise on evidence whose first volume was published in 1842—and his use of the term "in fault" (not "at fault") indicates that he had not fully disengaged himself from thinking of tort cases as governed by the writ system.

Shaw had associated tort cases with standards of civil liability, and by 1881, when Oliver Wendell Holmes Jr. published *The Common Law*, that association was cemented. In two chapters on torts, Holmes treated the field as a separate common law unit with its own rules and subdivided it into three standards of liability: intent, fault (which he called negligence), and what he called "act at peril" liability, when even persons who acted with the utmost care could be held accountable for injuries they caused. Holmes also argued that "act at peril" liability was anomalous, since it was not based on intent or fault, and that a negligence standard could be expected to govern most tort cases in the future.

The negligence principle and the expansion of tort law (1880–1950)

Holmes's 1881 characterization of tort law became the dominant approach of courts and commentators as the scope of American tort law dramatically expanded between the 1880s and the 1950s. Holmes's importance in the history of American tort law rests on his extensive reading of post–Civil War American cases involving civil injuries—he was the first scholar to organize those cases in a comprehensive fashion—and on judgments he made about the purposes of civil liability, which over time resonated with many of his contemporaries.

Over the course of the four years he spent updating the twelfth (1873) edition of James Kent's treatise *Commentaries on American Law*, Holmes noticed that civil injury cases were growing in number, that many of them involved accidents in which the parties had no preexisting relationships with one another, and that the theory of civil liability advanced in the cases was negligence on the part of the injuring party. Holmes concluded that negligence, in those cases, meant the neglect of a duty on the part of the defendant to act carefully so as not to injure the plaintiff. He noticed that this conception of a duty to act carefully had expanded from the original use of "duty" in civil cases, in which common law duties were associated only with particular statuses, such as innkeeper, municipality, or jailor, that were deemed to have special obligations to protect the public.

When exploding boilers threw debris that injured bystanders, or horses bolted into streets and injured pedestrians, or grass piled near railroad tracks caught fire from sparks set off by passing locomotives, Holmes noticed that courts granted relief to injured persons who could trace their damages to the negligent conduct of those maintaining the boilers, riding the horses, or servicing the railroad lines.

Holmes treated the expansion of cases grounded on a theory of negligent conduct as helping to define the boundaries of a new field of common law, torts. In addition to cases involving intentional injury, tort law now encompassed what Holmes called "modern negligence" cases, those encompassing the violation of a general duty to act carefully so as to not injure others. That general duty, Holmes felt, was owed "by all the world to all the world." Modern negligence was not simply the aggregate of older status duties owed by some persons to designated other persons (customers at an inn, users of a town's buildings or roads, those who encountered prisoners who had escaped from custody). Modern negligence was a general principle that "all the world" needed to take reasonable care to avoid injuring others.

When compared with earlier duties resting on status, modern negligence had the capacity to expand the scope of civil liability, but in Holmes's view it also served to narrow the definition of tortious injury. The writs associated with earlier civil injury cases appeared to anticipate that a third option had accompanied the requirement that civil injuries be intentionally or negligently inflicted, what Holmes called "act at peril" liability. English cases had held that when a landowner brought something on his property that was "liable to do mischief if it escapes," the landowner "must keep it in at his peril" and was responsible for any and all damage caused by its escape, even if it could not have been prevented through the exercise of reasonable care. The common illustration of this act at peril liability was the escape of cattle that ate neighbors' crops. And after a series of reservoirs used to collect water on estates burst their seams in the middle of the nineteenth century and flooded adjoining land, English courts placed liability on the owners even though they could not reasonably have prevented the water from escaping.

Although Holmes recognized the existence of act at peril liability in English cases, he thought the act at peril standard "peculiar." The "general principle of our law," he wrote in *The Common Law*, is that "loss from accident must lie where it falls." "Unless my act," he felt, "is of a nature to threaten others, unless under the circumstances a prudent man would have foreseen the possibility of harm, it is not more justifiable to make me indemnify my neighbor against the consequences, than . . . to compel me to insure him against lightning."

Holmes was not advocating the elimination of act at peril liability in civil injury cases, but he was interested in confining the scope of tort liability as the modern negligence principle expanded beyond status duties to a general duty of reasonable care. From the publication of *The Common Law* in 1881 through World War II, American courts and commentators generally agreed with him. As the United States became more populous, industrialized, and dominated by long-distance transportation, civil injuries, most of them emanating from industrial workplaces, highways, and railroads, increased dramatically. Tort law emerged as the principal mechanism for allocating the costs of those injuries, and modern negligence emerged as the principal basis of tort liability.

In the years between 1880 and 1950, the common law doctrines of tort law expanded their reach and variety. As those doctrines were applied across a larger range of cases, their expansion was not always commensurate with expanded liability in tort. In most jurisdictions, the tendency of late nineteenth- and early twentieth-century tort law was to limit act at peril liability: a showing of negligent or intentional conduct on the part of a defendant was normally a prerequisite for the recovery of damages.

And when negligence could be shown, it could limit as well as expand liability. Standards of reasonable conduct were applied against plaintiffs as well as defendants, so the doctrines of contributory negligence and assumption of risk could prevent plaintiffs who had unreasonably contributed to their injuries from recovering. Workers in dangerous jobs, for example, were denied recovery for the "ordinary risks" of those jobs on the theory that they could have chosen less hazardous occupations. And when an employee's negligent conduct injured another employee, the "fellow servant" doctrine prevented the injured employee from recovering against his or her employer, even if the employer could be shown to have tolerated or encouraged carelessness in employees.

Some status duties survived the acceptance of a general duty of care owed to all the world, and they operated, in certain contexts, to limit liability. Landowners were not treated as owing a general duty of care to anyone coming on their premises. They were held to have no obligation to take reasonable care to prevent injuries to trespassers, and their obligations to "licensees," a category that included social guests, did not include a duty to warn them about concealed risks on the premises. The conjunction of the doctrines of assumption of risk and contributory negligence with limited landowner duties meant that few bystander victims of automobile or railroad accidents could recover without showing that they had been unaware of the risks to themselves from close contact with cars or trains.

Not all the doctrinal developments in the years between 1880 and 1950 pointed in the direction of reduced liability. In several jurisdictions, judges responded to the perceived harshness of contributory negligence or the no-duty rule for injuries suffered by trespassers on land by creating exceptions to these doctrines.

8. A wreck on the Long Island Railroad in Bay Shore, New York, July 10, 1909, after a railroad train collided with the stationary car of another train. The nineteenth- and early twentieth-century increase in railroad traffic was accompanied by an increase in accidents to railroad employees and passengers. Until World War I, tort damage suits were typically the only way persons injured in railroad accidents could secure compensation for their injuries.

When young children stuck their hands in the turntable mechanisms used by trolley cars or fell into hazards on land near public highways, courts deemed them incapable of appreciating these risks and allowed them to recover damages. When motorists encountered pedestrians who had carelessly tried to cross roads and had time to avoid hitting them, they were said to have had "the last clear chance" to avoid injury, negating the contributory negligence of the pedestrians.

Of the doctrinal changes extending the scope of liability under negligence in the early and middle twentieth century, one was perhaps the most significant. It was the creation of a "duty" on the part of manufacturers of products made for mass consumption that ran beyond those "in privity" (having contractual relations) with the manufacturers to consumers and users of the products. In the leading case announcing this development, *MacPherson v. Buick Motor Co.* (1916), Judge Benjamin Cardozo of the highest court of New York said: "We have put aside the notion that the duty to safeguard life and limb . . . grows out of contract and nothing else. . . . We have put the source of the obligation in the law," meaning tort law.

Liability insurance and modifications of the common law tort system (1950–2000)

The expansion and refinement of the common law of torts, featuring modern negligence, was not perceived as a wholly successful response to the problem of redressing civil injury in late nineteenth- and early twentieth-century America. Dissatisfaction surfaced among enterprises that regularly found themselves defendants in tort suits and also among injured persons who turned to the tort system for relief.

In the first half of the twentieth century, three alternatives to the common law negligence regime as a mechanism for redressing civil injury surfaced. In chronological order, they were statutory

workers' compensation, proposals to replace portions of the
tort system with "no-fault" insurance coverage for categories of
accidents, and the judicial fashioning of a standard of "strict"
liability in a designated set of tort cases.

With the growth of industrialization, mass production, and heavy
machinery in the late nineteenth century, workplace accidents
increased. Because the fellow servant rule and the defenses of
contributory negligence and assumption of risk prevented many
injured workers from recovering damages for their injuries under
tort law, labor unions, which had emerged in the industrial sector,
lobbied for alternative compensation mechanisms. In response,
some state legislatures commissioned studies of injuries in
industrial workplaces, and out of those studies emerged the idea of
workers' compensation.

Workers' compensation was a statutorily required alternative to
tort law for certain categories of workplace injuries. Employers and
workers contributed to a fund out of which workplace injuries were
compensated, up to a limited amount, without regard to whether the
injury had been the result of negligence. Employers participating in
the system were immune from suit by their employees. By the 1920s,
workers' compensation statutes had been adopted in forty-three
states and had survived constitutional challenges.

Workers' compensation was only a partial substitute for the
common law tort system. It governed only some categories of
injuries, it only came into play when injuries occurred "within
the scope of employment" (a term defined by the worker's
compensation boards that administered claims), and it offered
limited damage awards. When workers were severely injured by
products they used at work and were able to establish that the
products had been negligently manufactured or designed and
that they had neither assumed the risks of using the products
or contributed to their injuries, they were sometimes better off
proceeding under tort law against the products' manufacturers.

As workers' compensation was emerging, another mechanism for responding to the increased cost of civil injuries had surfaced: third-party liability insurance, which was designed to protect persons who were exposed to lawsuits because they injured third parties. The practice of companies issuing contracts insuring others against risks had dated back to the eighteenth century in America but had been primarily confined to ship voyages and fires. By the late nineteenth century, some American companies began to offer "employer's insurance," designed as protection against employee suits. Soon that form of insurance was broadened to include protection against claims by passengers injured in railroad and streetcar accidents.

Liability insurance for the average citizen remained uncommon, however, until after World War II. Then, the ubiquity of automobile driving and the resultant increase in auto accidents involving strangers spawned the growth of third-party liability insurance. Collisions on the highways were a prime example.

As third-party liability insurance coverage became common for enterprises and automobile drivers, commentators began to perceive that its presence might have an effect on tort suits. A nineteenth-century objection to liability insurance had been that it would reduce incentives for policyholders to act safely toward others. Twentieth-century commentators revived that objection, reasoning that once liability insurance became widespread, enterprises and drivers would become less concerned with taking all reasonable steps to avoid tort liability, and thus the rules of common law negligence were less likely to affect their behavior.

The growth of liability insurance directly contributed to the sharp increase in suits against doctors for allegedly causing injury to their patients because of malpractice. Suits against physicians had been a regular feature of the tort system since the nineteenth century, and the medical profession complained of them persistently. In fact, though, there were few successful suits and few large damage awards against physicians before the 1960s. Then claims began to increase, with one study suggesting that between 1960 and 1968 they increased by 76 percent. The amount paid out for claims increased in New York state from approximately $46,000 to $104,000 between 1980 and 1984. The expansion of medical malpractice suits was directly related to the increase of liability insurance for physicians. It had been available since the 1920s but became pervasive in the 1960s, as insurance companies not only indemnified doctors against tort damages but assumed the defense of their cases. As virtually all doctors enrolled in liability insurance plans, it became more attractive to personal injury lawyers to file malpractice claims, hoping for settlements with insurance companies. Around the same time, the doctrine of charitable immunity for hospitals was abolished, providing medical malpractice plaintiffs with the opportunity to sue hospitals deemed vicariously liable for the malpractice of doctors affiliated with them.

Medical malpractice cases have achieved a certain notoriety because of the occasionally large verdicts, the volatility of malpractice insurance rates, and the difficulties some physician specialists—most prominently, obstetricians and gynecologists—have faced in obtaining insurance. But medical malpractice cases remain difficult for claimants to win: a successful suit requires not only a showing of malpractice but that the patient's condition was worsened by it. In addition, the widespread growth of health insurance has provided another mechanism for compensating injured persons for medical expenses.

The emergence of liability insurance also prompted the exploration of alternatives to the tort system of compensation. In 1965, two legal scholars proposed linking compulsory automobile insurance, which an increasing number of states had adopted since World War II, with a "no-fault" system of compensation for automobile injuries up to specified damage amounts. Their scheme required insurance companies to provide coverage for all motorists and to pay claims for injuries suffered in automobile accidents, up to designated limits, regardless of whether the party seeking compensation or other parties involved in the accident had been at fault. The goals of the plan were to remove many auto accident claims from the tort system and, theoretically, to enable insurance companies to calibrate the rates of their auto premiums more precisely. By 1976, sixteen states had adopted some form of no-fault automobile accident compensation.

In roughly the same time period, some state courts began to replace common law negligence with an alternative standard of liability in cases involving injuries from defective products. The courts and commentators who endorsed a "strict liability" standard in the defective products area reasoned that a certain percentage of socially useful, widely distributed products failed to perform—and injured users—because of flaws their manufacturers or distributors could not prevent through the use of ordinary care. In those circumstances, recovery for injuries caused by those products was not possible under the common law negligence regime.

That outcome seemed unfair and inefficient to an increasing number of courts in the 1960s and 1970s. Users of defective products commonly had less information about their dangers than manufacturers and distributors, and the enterprises that put the products on the market could insure themselves against potential injuries they might cause and either spread the costs of that insurance by raising the price of the products or withdraw products from the market if they were repeatedly dangerous. Judicial decisions imposing a standard of "strict" tort liability on manufacturers and distributors of defective products were grounded in those fairness and efficiency rationales. By the early 1970s, some commentators suggested that the entire area of defective products cases would eventually be governed by something resembling an "act at peril" standard of liability.

Developments in defective products cases were taken as evidence of a more general replacement of the common law of torts, replacing the emphasis on a negligence standard of liability with alternative systems for redressing civil injuries. Those systems, modeled on workers' compensation and featuring comprehensive insurance coverage, were expected to govern the treatment of a wide variety of injuries. In 1972, New Zealand instituted an accident compensation scheme under which residents waived their right to sue in tort for compensatory damages arising out of personal injury in exchange for compensation from a government-administered fund financed out of tax levies. Some American commentators hailed New Zealand's approach as the wave of the future. But by the close of the twentieth century, it was apparent that the anticipated replacement of the common law of torts with alternative compensation systems had not occurred. Despite its difficulties, the traditional regime, with its emphasis on a negligence standard of liability, was hard to displace, and alternative approaches were hard to implement.

An example was the judicial implementation of a standard of "strict" liability in torts cases. That standard had never been understood as the precise equivalent of act at peril liability. It only applied to products deemed "defective," not all products that injured someone, and the meaning of "defect" was a term of art, to be formulated over a range of cases. Some dangerous products, such as sharp knives, were treated as "unavoidably unsafe" because their riskiness had social utility, and sometimes products with what were termed "open and obvious" risks could be misused. Recovery was barred in such instances: not every injury caused by a product rendered the maker of the product accountable.

As courts began implementing the standard of "strict liability" in defective products cases, their analysis came to resemble judicial definitions of "reasonable care" in negligence cases. Commonly employed criteria from the negligence regime, such as weighing the costs of preventing injuries from the products against the likelihood that a product manufactured or designed in a particular way would cause severe injury, came to inform judicial definitions of a "defect." An example was defectively designed products, for which part of the burden for plaintiffs seeking to establish a defective design was showing that a "reasonable alternative design" existed that was safer and not prohibitively costly. The "reasonableness" of a design was determined on the basis of negligence criteria. As analogies from negligence crept into the law of defective products, it became clear that "strict" liability in defective products cases resembled negligence more than act at peril liability. By the end of the twentieth century, the *Restatement Third* of tort law, an authoritative summary of the field promulgated by the American Law Institute, identified only one area of defective products cases as being governed by a "stricter" standard of liability than negligence, that in which a unit in a manufactured product line failed to perform. Cases involving defectively designed products and cases in which warnings on products were inadequate, the *Restatement Third* found, were governed by the equivalent of a negligence standard.

The pervasiveness of liability insurance did not, in the end, result in alternative compensation systems displacing tort law in the last two decades of the twentieth century. The growth of no-fault automobile accident plans slowed after 1976, with some states repealing their coverage. Moreover, American no-fault compensation schemes had never fully replaced tort law: they had been limited to automobile accidents and only governed damages up to a certain threshold. For other sorts of injuries, and more severe automobile accident damages, the option to sue in tort was always retained. Meanwhile, strict liability in the area of defective products became so riddled with doctrines brought over from the negligence regime as to widen the scope of that regime rather than emerging as an alternative to it.

Thus, one is tempted to treat the narrative history of civil injury and tort law in America as coming full cycle. Tort law's identity as a discrete field was initially associated with the rise and expansion of negligence as a standard of civil liability. Then, as dissatisfaction with some of the limiting effects of negligence surfaced, alternatives to tort law as a compensation mechanism were considered. Over time, it has been difficult to disengage those alternatives from negligence doctrines, with the result that common law suits in negligence remain the principal way Americans have sought civil redress for injuries inflicted on them by others.

But the history of American tort law has been neither that cyclical nor that straightforward. Identifying which injuries qualify for relief under the tort system, developing and applying standards of civil liability, and evaluating the performance of the tort system against alternative compensation systems, including workers' compensation, have been recurrent and formidable tasks. History suggests that the problem of redressing civil injury has been, and will remain, a central challenge for America.

Chapter 8
Legal education and the legal profession

The importance of law and legal documents in the formation of the American republic ensured that lawyers would be culturally significant figures in the new nation's early history. Moreover, the territorial and economic growth of the United States in the first half of the nineteenth century was facilitated by legal developments and created a demand for legal services. This meant that people with legal training would play important roles in the process by which America evolved from a former British colony to a world power. But the need for lawyers in America was not matched by a systematic development of institutions for educating prospective members of the legal profession or processes for certifying their qualifications. Instead American legal education, and standards for entering the profession, remained rudimentary and informal until after the Civil War.

The colonial and revolutionary years

When British colonies were formed in America in the seventeenth and early eighteenth centuries, they came with charters—documents that set out the terms of governance in each colony—and in some instances with codes: promulgations of criminal and civil laws within their borders. At the time colonial British settlement was taking place, the English legal profession had subdivided itself into barristers (lawyers who argued cases in court), solicitors (lawyers who gave out-of-court advice and solicited clients for barristers), and what were called "attorneys." Those classes of lawyers had different training and performed different functions. The function of attorneys was simply to read and decipher legal documents: they were the equivalent of what today would be called paralegals. They neither represented clients nor appeared in court and were often employed by barristers or solicitors.

In early colonial America most of the persons professing some familiarity with legal documents were attorneys. Few British solicitors or barristers had incentives to migrate to America, and none of the institutions where they received training initially existed in the colonies. In England, barristers were typically graduates of universities who attached themselves to "Inns of Court," groups where barristers ate meals and discussed professional issues. After becoming affiliated with an Inn, a prospective barrister then needed to become associated with an office of barristers, called a chambers, to which solicitors would bring cases to be argued in court. Solicitors typically did not attend universities: they received on-the-job training in a solicitor's office. They needed to become conversant with the law of various subjects in order to render advice and determine whether their clients would profit through litigation. There were no Inns of Court in the British colonies, and the barrister/solicitor distinction quickly disappeared. Although courts and court proceedings quickly became important features of life in the colonies, persons could appear in court without legal representation, and most judges lacked legal training.

It was not until the middle of the eighteenth century that a critical mass of people to form the basis of a legal profession had emerged in the British colonies. By the 1750s creole elites—second- and third-generation residents of the colonies whose families had originally come from Great Britain—lived in the principal cities of colonial America: Boston, New York, Philadelphia, and

Charleston, South Carolina. Members of the legal profession were drawn heavily from these elites, who also played a decisive role in American independence. They were members of the Continental Congress, which produced the Declaration of Independence and subsequently the U.S. Constitution. They included George Washington, John Adams, Thomas Jefferson, John Jay, James Madison, and Alexander Hamilton.

All of those men had received some training in law. Neither Washington nor Madison formally entered the legal profession, but each, as part of his education, had read some law books. An acquaintance with law was regarded as part of the education of male members of the gentry class in the British colonies. The owners of estates typically needed some practical understanding of legal affairs in managing their properties, so law, along with such subjects as moral philosophy, the natural sciences, and the history of ancient Greece and Rome, came to be among the offerings to which young male members of elites were exposed to as they grew up.

Jefferson, Jay, and Hamilton had also attended some lectures in law, which had come to be offered at colleges or "proprietary" schools in the eighteenth century. Proprietary schools were for-profit institutions created by lawyers and judges who gave lectures for students aspiring to the legal profession. Proprietary schools were not affiliated with colleges or universities, who sometimes offered lectures in law to undergraduates. The College of William and Mary, where Jefferson and John Marshall (later chief justice of the United States) studied, was an example of a college offering law lectures, as was Kings College in New York, where Hamilton was a pupil. The Litchfield School of Law in Connecticut was the foremost proprietary school of the eighteenth century. Law lectures were designed as professional training, but attendance at them was not a requirement for entering the legal profession.

In fact, the predominant way residents of the British colonies trained for the legal profession was as apprentices. They secured space in an existing law office, where, in exchange for performing clerical tasks, they were given the opportunity to read legal treatises and, if they were fortunate, to receive some scholarly or practical instruction from the resident lawyers. By the 1770s, William Blackstone's summary of English common law, *Commentaries on the Law of England*, was widely available in the colonies, and it became part of many apprentices' instruction. After a period of apprenticeship, an aspiring lawyer sought admission to the "bar" of a particular colony. (The term "bar," which initially referred to the space dividing lawyers in a courtroom from spectators, eventually came to designate professional associations of people who were qualified to practice law.) By the time an apprentice was examined, he had typically become associated with a firm of lawyers. Admission to the bars of colonies (and subsequently states) was initially not a demanding process, consisting of a brief oral examination, often administered by a close acquaintance of the applicant.

In 1776, the consequences of acquiring legal training in colonial British America suddenly became very significant. When members of the Continental Congress decided to sever formal ties with the British Empire and to create a new government composed of a confederation of former colonies, now designated independent states, those steps had been justified in legal documents. The founding acts of the American Revolution—the Declaration of Independence, the written constitutions of the new states, the Articles of Confederation, the Constitution of the United States—all took the form of written legal documents justifying the actions of former citizens of the British Empire and setting forth the structure of the new institutions that would govern America. Americans identified themselves, in their founding documents, as persons rejecting monarchy and parliamentary supremacy, affirming the principles of natural rights and sovereignty in the people at large, and declaring their adherence to the ideal of a society ruled by law rather than men and to fundamental principles written in constitutions. From independence on,

Americans would describe themselves as a people governed by law. This meant that lawyers would be intimately involved with American public life and politics.

Legal education and professional roles in the nineteenth century

A high percentage of the men involved in the framing of the Declaration of Independence and the Constitution were members of the legal profession, as were a high percentage of the members of Congress and state legislatures in the early American republic. The close association of legal training with public service, and of political accountability with the selection of judges, were products of Americans' commitment in the late eighteenth century to written constitutions and republican government. Over the course of the nineteenth century, however, demands for legal services also emerged in the private sector.

As the territory and population of the United States dramatically expanded in the first half of the nineteenth century, lawyers participated in every stage of that process. They advised the commercial enterprises that sprang up in both agriculture and industry over the course of the nineteenth century. They served on the legislatures of states that built canals and granted land to railroads. They were members of Congress when it disposed of newly acquired public lands. When new states came into the Union, bar associations were created in those states: as the population of the states grew, so did the number of their residents qualified to practice law. It became clear that the major route to public office in nineteenth-century America was through the practice of law.

Despite the growing demand for lawyers that territorial expansion and population growth created, the traditional mechanisms for training persons for the legal profession did not change significantly up to the Civil War. Apprenticeship remained the principal way to enter the profession, and the standards for admission to state bars actually declined in the first half of the nineteenth century, with some states permitting anyone who was a resident of a state to qualify for the bar. Although one might have thought that the demand for lawyers would have resulted in more university-affiliated or proprietary law schools being established, that was not the case in the first half of the nineteenth century. Most law schools of either type failed to stay in operation for more than a few years: in 1840 the United States had only nine law schools, with a total of 345 students, affiliated with colleges or universities. In addition, states began to abolish apprenticeship requirements. In 1800, fourteen of nineteen states had established a period of apprenticeship as a prerequisite for applying to their bars; by 1840, only eleven of thirty states required apprenticeships, and by 1860 only nine of thirty-nine.

What did aspiring lawyers study as preparation for admission to a bar? Those who attended law schools would be exposed to lectures that amounted to overviews of legal subjects. By the second decade of the nineteenth century, treatises collecting cases and commentary in particular legal subjects had begun to appear, the best known of which, James Kent's *Commentaries on American Law*, was the product of lectures Kent had given at Columbia College. Kent's *Commentaries* were widely adopted, and Joseph Story, a justice of the Supreme Court who also taught at Harvard Law School beginning in 1827, began issuing treatises on a variety of legal subjects in the 1830s. By the Civil War, students attending a law school could expect that the lectures offered there would likely be replicated in a treatise. Law schools also offered "moot courts," practice exercises in courtroom advocacy, with students and professors serving as judges.

Students who chose to serve as apprentices often had less systematic preparation. Sometimes they were simply given clerical tasks in an office, a version of practical training. Often lawyers would recommend that they study Blackstone's *Commentaries*.

The published reporting of state and federal cases remained rudimentary for most of the first half of the nineteenth century, but some states, such as New York, and the U.S. Supreme Court published reported decisions during that period. There were thus some opportunities for apprentices to "learn the law" from books. But many simply served as clerks in an office until they felt capable of taking a bar examination.

Given the widespread demand for legal services in nineteenth-century America, traditional barriers to entry into the legal profession were difficult to maintain. The barrister/solicitor distinction in England, which rested on prospective barristers being accepted to one of the Inns of Court, had functioned to exclude persons who were not graduates of English universities or did not have social connections from becoming barristers, and thus being permitted to argue cases in court. The distinction may have been instinctively alien to republican ideology in America and stood in the way of rapidly expanding the pool of lawyers, and thus never took root. By the outset of the Civil War, in several states nearly anyone who wanted to become a lawyer could do so with a minimum of professional training.

As the Civil War drew to a close, that situation had not changed. Law courses were still offered at only a few universities, and no formal connection had been established between attendance at a law school, whether proprietary or university-affiliated, and admission to a bar. Law schools were essentially alternative ways of becoming exposed to the materials one might study as an apprentice. When Oliver Wendell Holmes Jr., an 1861 graduate of Harvard College, matriculated at Harvard Law School in 1864, his courses consisted of lectures on various subjects, plus some moot court exercises. There were no requirements for admission and no examinations. After taking courses for three semesters, Holmes apparently thought he had learned enough from lectures; he stopped attending them and in early 1866 associated himself with a law office in Boston. He was nonetheless awarded a law degree from Harvard in June 1866. His admission to the Massachusetts bar was not a rigorous process: when he took the bar examination in March 1867, it consisted only of oral questions and was administered to him by a close acquaintance.

In a critique of his experiences at Harvard Law School, written three years later, Holmes said that its only requirements were attendance at a sufficient number of lectures and matriculation fees, and Harvard had been "doing something every year . . . to discourage real students." A law faculty member published a defense of the school, but Holmes was right. Harvard at the time was simply organizing materials of legal study for persons who would otherwise be doing it for themselves. Twenty years after Holmes's comments, the situation at Harvard had changed dramatically.

As large-scale industrialization began to take hold in America later in the nineteenth century, the demand for legal services continued to increase, and new patterns of immigration resulted in some different classes of entrants into the legal profession. Immigrants from southern and eastern Europe came to the United States in greater numbers after the Civil War, and by the close of the century, second-generation members of some immigrant families were aspiring to practice law. Proprietary law schools increased in urban centers, some of them offering night classes, and applications to the bar from second-generation immigrants increased.

With the appointment in 1869 of Charles Eliot as president and, a year later, of C. C. Langdell as dean of the law school, Harvard made a decisive turn toward making its professional schools more rigorous. By the close of Langdell's deanship in 1895, Harvard Law School had instituted admission requirements, signaled that it was inclined to admit only college graduates, begun regular, graded examinations, and offered degrees only to students with satisfactory academic performances. The implicit message of those changes was to certify the professional qualifications of Harvard graduates.

As additional law schools followed Harvard's shift from providing an alternative to apprenticeship preparation to serving as a postundergraduate institution whose mission was to certify the professional status of its graduates, comparable shifts took place within the legal profession. When the American Bar Association (ABA) was founded in 1878, its first priority was increasing standards within the legal profession by tightening the state requirements for bar admission. Over the course of the next fifty years, however, the ABA shifted its emphasis, increasingly seeking to have law schools function as institutions that could verify the ability of entrants into the profession. This shift eventually resulted in graduation from an ABA-certified law school being

9. Abraham Lincoln maintained a law office in the Posey Building in Shawneetown, Illinois. Lincoln had a general practice, representing anyone from farmers to railroad corporations in the Illinois courts. He was recognized for his skill at appealing to juries through "plain and simple" statements of his clients' positions.

made a prerequisite for admission to a state's bar, a situation which currently exists in nearly all states. (Some have continued to allow applicants who have "read for the bar," a term designating apprentices.) Meanwhile, the Association of American Law Schools (AALS), which spun off from the ABA in 1915, identified its primary mission as improving the quality of legal education by making the law school experience more uniform.

Legal education in the twentieth century

Between the opening of the twentieth century and World War II, a number of issues relating to the structure and function of American law schools were debated within the ABA, the AALS, and universities. By the 1950s, those issues had been resolved in favor of a model of interaction among undergraduate institutions, law schools, and the legal profession that remains largely in place in the twenty-first century.

One set of issues involved requirements for admission and graduation, curricular offerings, and methods of instruction. The study of law had not been decisively linked with postundergraduate education during the nineteenth and early twentieth centuries: as late as World War II some law schools did not require an undergraduate degree as a prerequisite for admission. After 1950, however, American law schools all became postundergraduate institutions, requiring that applicants possess college degrees, making three years of study a prerequisite for a degree, and offering courses that were rarely offered to undergraduates. Moreover, many law school catalogs in the 1950s noted that the primary pedagogic emphasis of law courses was teaching students how to "think like lawyers." In most law schools the "Socratic method" of instruction, introduced at Harvard in the late nineteenth century, had become the norm. It consisted of professors guiding students through a close analysis of appellate cases with a question-and-answer dialogue. The materials of legal study were, in the main, casebooks, with students, under questioning, being expected to extract the legal doctrines embedded in cases. Grades were based on one comprehensive examination per course that asked students to analyze hypothetical cases. Class rankings and membership in the student-edited law journals that published legal scholarship were determined by grades. Grade performance on examinations became the primary method of identifying the eligibility of law school graduates for legal jobs in the private and public sectors, judicial clerkships, and positions in the legal academy.

In the same period, the relationship among universities, law schools, and the professional accreditation standards of the ABA, the AALS, and state bar associations was transformed. In the first three decades of the twentieth century, universities either merged with proprietary schools or started their own law schools, and proprietary schools decreased. Meanwhile, the AALS took steps to accredit new law schools and to oversee the performance of its members, and the ABA began to involve itself in the process by establishing accreditation requirements. The final step in the process was the adoption by state bar associations of a requirement that to qualify for bar membership an applicant had to be a graduate of an accredited law school. Taken together, those developments marked the virtual end of proprietary law schools and of the option of preparing for admission to a bar by reading for the law outside of a law school setting.

Students entering law school after the 1950s found the admissions process, which came to include a standardized law school admissions test as well as a review of undergraduate grades and recommendations, increasingly competitive. They also found that a hierarchy of law schools had been established, with law schools in the top tier drawing their students from all regions of the nation and placing them widely. Law schools had emerged as the primary credentialing institutions of the legal profession, with a law school's reputation and a student's grades serving as proxies for creating employment opportunities.

The changes that took place in legal education during the first half of the twentieth century addressed the principal challenge of the American legal profession for much of its early history: how to maintain quality controls amid a rapidly growing demand for legal services. As law schools emerged as credentialing institutions, states tightened their requirements for admission to bars. Instead of admitting nearly anyone who had sufficient connections and was able to read for the law, state bars used law school admission requirements, grades, and bar examinations as barriers to entry into the profession.

The legal profession in the twentieth century

While law schools were being transformed, and the relation between law school attendance and credentialing for the profession was being made more explicit, the legal profession, including its judicial branch, were also undergoing decisive changes. As entrepreneurship changed its focus in the late nineteenth and twentieth centuries, new demands for legal services emerged, changing the character of American law firms. All of the major entrepreneurial innovations after the Civil War were facilitated and perpetuated by lawyers. Lawyers arranged the mergers between industrial competitors that created the giant holding companies of the late nineteenth and early twentieth centuries. Lawyers helped their clients secure patents, copyright inventions, and establish protection for their innovations in intellectual property. Lawyers advised movie studios, actors, and participants in the record industry. Lawyers were deeply involved in the movements for greater racial and gender equality and in the protection of the civil rights and civil liberties of minorities. Lawyers provided representation for the increasing number of persons who came into contact with the criminal justice system.

The size and composition of law firms reflected those changes. As the demand for "out of court" representation (advice to

10. **Professor John Calvin Jeffries Jr. teaches a first-year class in criminal law at the University of Virginia School of Law. Most professors teaching first-year law classes continue to employ the Socratic method, a mode of pedagogy that dates back to the late nineteenth century. It seeks to unravel the reasoning of appellate court opinions by posing a series of questions to students.**

clients who seek to avoid running afoul of the law in their activities) increased with the expansion of business activity, law firms became larger and the practice of their members more specialized. By the 1980s, some law firms in major cities had more than five hundred members. Larger law firms began to open branch offices in other cities, and in the early decades of the twenty-first century, law firms began to merge with one another, creating "superfirms" with multiple branches. As law firms got bigger and their work more specialized, they developed an appetite for hiring junior associates on a salary basis, working them very long hours, and billing their work at rates that exceeded their salary levels. During the last decade of the twentieth century, the salaries of entry-level lawyers joining large firms increased dramatically, but the incomes of partners in these firms increased even more.

Then, multiple shocks hit the law firm market in the twenty-first century. The economic downturn brought about by the 2001 attack on the World Trade Center took years to absorb, and just as the prospects of law firms were again appearing robust, the fiscal crisis of 2008 dramatically cut into law firm business, since much of it had been tied to work in the financial industries and the corporate real estate sector. Firms that had been hiring large numbers of recent law school graduates began to reduce their hiring or defer the starting time for graduates with job offers. The number of graduates from law schools who had secured jobs by graduation began to decline. Meanwhile, the cost of law school tuition increased markedly in the first decade of the century, such that many law students had to accumulate significant debt by the time they graduated. The burdens placed on students by high debt and diminished job prospects were considerable, resulting in a noticeable decline in applications to law school, which had been on a steeply rising curve since the 1990s. This episode reveals how closely law schools and law firms have come to be linked in contemporary America: prosperity or its absence in the law firm market quickly has effects on the financial health of law schools.

The one institution in the legal profession that has been comparatively unscathed by the economic volatility of the late twentieth and twenty-first century has been the judiciary. Judges have always held salaried positions in America, and entry into the judicial profession has been closely tied to politics. Courts have always been important institutions in American society, and since World War II there has been a noticeable increase in the litigation of disputes, only partially because of the constitutional obligation to provide all criminal defendants with representation. One might have expected that with the increase in litigation and consequent pressure on court dockets, states and the federal government would have increased the number of judgeships. But judicial appointments have not kept pace with the increase in the courts' business, primarily because elected political officials continue to play a decisive role in the appointments process. Although judgeships continue to be regarded as prestigious within the legal profession, the widening gap between the salary structure of judges and those of large-firm practitioners and legal academics, from which candidates for judgeships have traditionally been drawn, has combined with the heavy demands of court dockets to make the judicial sector of the legal profession perhaps less coveted than it once was.

Despite its current difficulties, the legal profession, including its educational and judicial sectors, remains at the very center of American life, a place that promises financial rewards, influence, and stimulating work to many of its members and that has been intimately involved with the central issues of American society and politics, and will continue to be.

Epilogue

This book may be taken as an effort to demonstrate how much of American history can be seen as connected to law and legal institutions. Legal documents, in the form of royal and proprietary charters and codes of conduct, framed the initial settlement of British North America. The institutions of royal governors and colonial assemblies structured the lives of colonial settlers, for better and for worse. Legal documents announced the independence of the American colonies from the British empire, created the forms of government adopted by the newly created American states, defined the powers of the first federal government in America, and modified that government in the Constitution of the United States.

Law, in the form of treaties, court proceedings, and eventually constitutional decisions, defined the shifting relationship between European settlers and native tribes in America. Legal doctrines and policies formed the justifications for the dispossession of American Indians from their tribal lands, the removal of tribes westward as European settlers sought to occupy more land, and eventually the confinement of tribes on reservations as wards of the federal government. Law was equally responsible for the emergence and growth of the enslavement of African Americans in North America. State laws legitimated the initial practice of slavery in the southern Atlantic coastal colonies; associated the status of enslavement with skin color and African ancestry; and codified the practices necessary to sustain a system in which enslaved persons were considered property and enslavement was considered a condition precluding a person's rights to most human freedoms. Eventually, law not only justified the spread of slavery into some portions of the territory acquired by the United States between 1803 and 1853 but also, in the *Dred Scott* decision, prohibited the federal government's abolition of slavery in its territories as unconstitutional.

Law undergirded the ways individuals and families acquired, transferred, and devised real and personal property. Legal entities and devices, such as franchises, partnerships, corporations, and easements, facilitated the opening up of the American continent and the movement of goods and people from east to west. Lawyers invoked copyrights and patents to protect authors, inventors, and entrepreneurs in emerging markets. Lawyers created instruments such as trusts and holding companies to encourage the mergers of competitors in the industrial sector. The federal government, states, and municipalities subsidized the building of turnpikes, canals, and railroads and doled out radio and television licenses and cable franchises.

Legal institutions transformed domestic relations and created a system for compensating civil injuries. The roles of men, women, and children in households were redefined by judicial decisions and legislation. The status of marriage, divorce, abortion, and illegitimacy was altered, over time, by courts and legislatures. Eventually, same-sex relationships between consenting adults, including marriages, were legitimized in some states. Meanwhile, tort law existed as a mechanism by which people injured through the intentional conduct or "fault" (negligence) of others could seek redress for their injuries. As more people came into contact with mechanisms of an industrializing society that could injure them— railroads, street cars, automobiles, machines in factories, defectively manufactured or designed products—doctrines of the law of torts were modified to help provide some compensation for such injuries.

The area in which the field of law can arguably be seen most clearly responding to and shaping social conduct was the realm of criminal activity. It was law that defined that activity in the first place, typically in the form of state legislation. Initially, many criminalized offenses in America were connected to public morality: adultery, fornication, sodomy, sexual molestation of minors. Because of the moral dimensions of crimes, early punishments emphasized social stigma (whippings, brandings, placement in stocks) rather than incarceration. Official police forces were late to materialize, not appearing until the nineteenth century. As definitions of crime shifted from morals offenses to threats to property and persons, punishment shifted toward the incarceration (and prospective rehabilitation) of criminals, on the theory that such threats could be reduced if criminals were removed from society. For much of American history, the focus of criminal law was on defining crimes and convicting criminals rather than the threat of excessive criminalization or too zealous enforcement by the state. But in the mid-twentieth century, the emphasis dramatically shifted, resulting in the judicial creation of constitutional safeguards for persons accused of crimes. Then, after a series of U.S. Supreme Court decisions had imposed constraints on the activities of both police and prosecutors, emphasis shifted again, as political figures and the public became fearful that courts were turning criminals loose on legal technicalities and that "law and order" was consequently breaking down. The result, mirrored in longer sentences and less judicial discretion to modify legislatively enforced punishments, was a marked increase in the number of people incarcerated. The history of American criminal law thus provides an apt illustration of the reciprocal relationship between law and its social context. Changes in both the doctrines and the policies of criminal law have been responses not only to perceptions about the nature and state of criminal activity and but also to factors that have helped shape these perceptions.

Of all the evidence demonstrating the role of law as a central force in the history of American culture, the most visible has been the status of the legal profession itself. Since the early settlements in colonial British America, a knowledge of law has been associated with governing institutions, politics, and influence in community affairs. Initially, partly because of the absence of training institutions such as law schools or the equivalent of the Inns of Court, this association in people's minds did not arise from the United States having a community of highly trained lawyers. Rather, possibly due to republican ideology, there was a strong demand for persons with some smattering of legal knowledge, which was often acquired informally. Eventually, state bar associations and law schools and, later, national organizations such as the ABA and the AALS became involved with the process of professional certification. This did not take place until the twentieth century, but in the preceding years lawyers had nonetheless exerted a great deal of influence in business affairs and politics, and the courts had emerged as primary mechanisms for resolving disputes.

There has always been a certain amount of antagonism toward members of the legal profession in America, and long-standing support for the ideal of a rule of law has been matched by a long tradition of civil disobedience that has sought to appeal to principles of fairness, justice, and equality that transcend legal rules. But it has only been very recently that a diminished market for legal services has been coupled with a diminished trust among Americans in their public officials, most of whom are lawyers. Whether the current very low standing of members of Congress and other public officials will combine with reduced prospects for law school graduates to shift the status of the legal profession from its position of centrality in American life remains to be seen. If so, that change would be a radical departure from that profession's role in American history.

References

Chapter 1

Alexis de Tocqueville statement from *Democracy in America*, ed.
　　J. P. Mayer (Garden City, N.Y.: Doubleday, 1969), 339, 324.
The letter from Madison to Monroe was written in April 1824. It is
　　quoted in Annie H. Abel, "The History of Events Resulting in
　　Indian Consolidation West of the Mississippi," in *Annual Report of
　　the American Historical Association for 1906*, 2 vols. (Washington,
　　D.C.: General Printing Office, 1908), 1:255.
Johnson v. McIntosh, 8 Wheat 543 (1823); *Cherokee Nation v. Georgia*,
　　5 Pet. 1 (1831); *Worcester v. Georgia*, 6 Pet. 515 (1832); *Lone Wolf v.
　　Hitchcock*, 187 U.S. 553 (1903).
The 1934 newspaper editorial is Joseph C. Harsch, "Star of Self-Rule
　　for American Indian Rises," *Christian Science Monitor*, April 11,
　　1934, 7.
The Cayuga Nation's lawsuit against New York state was decided in
　　Cayuga Indian Nation of New York v. Pataki, 165 F. Supp. 2d 266
　　(N.D.N.Y. 2001).

Chapter 2

Dred Scott v. Sandford, 19 How. 393 (1857).

Chapter 3

Kelo v. City of New London, 529 U.S. 469 (2005).

Chapter 4

The first authoritative Supreme Court decision treating film speech
in motion pictures as being protected by the First Amendment
was *Joseph Burstyn Inc. v. Wilson*, 343 U.S. 495 (1952). In an
earlier case, *United States v. Paramount Pictures*, 334 U.S. 131
(1948), Justice William O. Douglas's majority opinion had stated
that "motion pictures, like newspapers and radio, are included in
the press whose freedom is guaranteed by the First Amendment"
(334 U.S. at 166), but that statement was not necessary to the
Paramount Pictures decision.

The Court's conclusion that the FCC could regulate "indecent" content
on radio and network television broadcasts came in *FCC v. Pacifica
Foundation*, 438 U.S. 726 (1978).

The 1989 case in which the Court held that Congress could not
constitutionally restrict the transmission of "indecent" commercial
telephone messages was *Sable Communications, Inc. v. FCC*, 492
U.S. 115 (1989).

The 1996 and 2000 cases in which the Court invalidated provisions of
the 1992 Cable Television Consumer Protection and Competition
Act and the Telecommunications Act of 1996, both of which
required cable providers to block or "scramble" indecent
programming, as opposed to segregating it in late evening hours,
were *Denver Area Educational Telecommunications Consortium
v. FCC*, 518 U.S. 727 (1996) and *United States v. Playboy
Entertainment Group*, 529 U.S. 803 (2000).

The 1994 and 1997 decisions upholding the FCC's "must carry" rules
for cable providers were *Turner Broadcasting System Inc. v. FCC*,
512 U.S. 622 (1994) and *Turner Broadcasting System v. FCC*, 520
U.S. 180 (1997).

The 1997 and 2004 decisions striking down Congress's efforts to
regulate "indecent" and "patently offensive" communications on the
Internet were *Reno v. American Civil Liberties Union*, 521 U.S. 844
(1997), and *Ashcroft v. American Civil Liberties Union*, 535 U.S.
564 (2004).

Chapter 5

Three articles in *The Cambridge History of Law in America*, ed. Michael
Grossberg and Christopher Tomlins, 3 vols. (New York: Cambridge
University Press, 2008), provide a good background on the evolution

of criminal law and theories of rehabilitation and punishment from the seventeenth through the twentieth centuries. See Michael Meranze, "Penalty and the Colonial Project: Crime, Punishment, and the Regulation of Morals in Early America," 1:178–210; Elizabeth Dale, "Criminal Justice in the United States, 1790–1920: A Government of Laws or Men?" 2:133–67; and Michael Willrich, "Criminal Justice in the United States," 3:195–231. For additional overviews, see Lawrence M. Friedman, *Law in America: A Short History* (New York: Random House, 2002), 73–122, and Kermit L. Hall and Peter Karsten, *The Magic Mirror: Law in American History* (New York: Oxford University Press, 2009), 187–207.

Chapter 6

For more detail on the inaccuracy, as it applied to colonial America, of Blackstone's characterization of domestic householding as an extended domain of hierarchical relationships, see Holly Brewer, "The Transformation of Domestic Law," in the *Cambridge History*, 1:292–313.

The quotation from James Kent is from his *Commentaries on American Law*, 4 vols. (New York: O. Halsted, 1826), 2:120.

The Supreme Court decisions invalidating restrictions on the distribution of birth control information to married couples or individuals were *Griswold v. Connecticut*, 381 U.S. 479 (1965), and *Eisenstadt v. Baird*, 405 U.S. 438. The decision invalidating restrictions on interracial marriage was *Loving v. Virginia*, 388 U.S. 1 (1967). The decision invalidating complete bans on the choice of a woman to terminate a pregnancy was *Roe v. Wade*, 410 U.S. 113 (1973).

The 1986 case in which the Court sustained the constitutionality of state laws criminalizing consensual same-sex intimate conduct was *Bowers v. Hardwick*, 478 U.S. 186. The *Bowers* decision was overruled in *Lawrence v. Texas*, 539 U.S. 539 (2003).

Chapter 7

The 1850 Massachusetts case involving the dogfight was *Brown v. Kendall*, 6 Cush. 282 (1850). The quotations from that case come from pp. 294–95 and 295–96 (italics in original).

The reference to Holmes's chapters on torts in *The Common Law* is to Oliver Wendell Holmes, *The Common Law* (Boston: Little Brown, 1881), 71–147.

The quotations on act at peril liability in nineteenth-century English cases are from *Fletcher v. Rylands*, 1 L. R. Exch. 265, 279 (1866).

The "general principle of our law" quotation from Holmes is from *Common Law*, 94–96.

The quotation from Cardozo is from *MacPherson v. Buick Motor Co.*, 217 N.Y. 382, 390 (1916).

The 1965 book proposing no-fault automobile accident insurance was Robert E. Keeton and Jeffrey O'Connell, *Basic Protection for the Traffic Victim* (Boston: Little, Brown, 1965).

Chapter 8

The figures on university-affiliated law schools and apprenticeship requirements in the early nineteenth century are taken from Robert Stevens, *Law School: Legal Education in America from the 1850s to the 1980s* (Chapel Hill: University of North Carolina Press, 1983), 7–8.

Holmes's comment about Harvard Law School is in [Oliver Wendell Holmes Jr.], "Harvard Law School," *American Law Review* 5 (1870), 177.

Further reading

The best current anthology of useful scholarship on topics in American legal history is Michael Grossberg and Christopher Tomlins, *The Cambridge History of Law in America*, 3 vols. (New York: Cambridge University Press, 2008). Several articles in this anthology provide additional information on the subjects covered in this book.

Chapter 1

I employ the term "Amerindian" in this chapter, and in G. Edward White, *Law in American History*, vol. 1, *From the Colonial Years through the Civil War* (New York: Oxford University Press, 2012), to reflect the fact that the earliest European visitors to North America erroneously believed that they had reached the Indian subcontinent and designated the aboriginal tribes they encountered "Indian" inhabitants of what they subsequently came to call "America." For accessible overviews of the dispossession and marginalization of tribes over the course of American history, see Stuart Banner, *How the Indians Lost Their Land* (Cambridge, Mass.: Harvard University Press, 2005), and Frank Pommershein, *Broken Landscape* (New York: Oxford University Press, 2008). In the *Cambridge History*, Katherine A. Hermes, "The Law of Native Americans, to 1815," 1:32–62, and David E. Wilkins, "Federal Policy, Western Movement, and Consequences for Indigenous People, 1790–1920," 2:204–44, provide more detail on the themes addressed in the chapter.

Chapter 2

Two of the essays on the legal history of slavery in the *Cambridge History* are particularly useful compilations of the numerous ways the practice of African American enslavement was codified, implemented, and justified by common law decisions, state statutes, and interpretations of the Constitution. See Sally E. Hadden, "The Fragmented Laws of Slavery in the Colonial and Revolutionary Eras," 1:253–87, and Ariela Gross, "Slavery, Antislavery, and the Coming of the Civil War," 2:280–312. Additional treatments of the law of African-American enslavement can be found in Thomas D. Morris, *Southern Slavery and the Law 1619-1860* (Chapel Hill: University of North Carolina Press, 1996), and Kermit L. Hall and Peter Karsten, *The Magic Mirror: Law in American History* (New York: Oxford University Press, 2009), 142–67.

Chapter 3

The best overview of evolving ideas of property rights and their regulation in American history is Gregory S. Alexander, *Commodity and Propriety: Competing Visions of Property in American Legal Thought* (Chicago: University of Chicago Press, 1998). Although primarily concerned with constitutional issues, James W. Ely Jr., *The Guardian of Every Other Right: A Constitutional History of Property Rights*, 3rd ed. (New York: Oxford University Press, 2008), contains a helpful overview of changing attitudes toward the relationship of property holding and acquisition to governmental regulation. William Novak, *The People's Welfare: Law and Regulation in Nineteenth-Century America* (Chapel Hill: University of North Carolina Press, 1996), demonstrates the persistence of promotional and regulatory theories of landownership in the nineteenth century.

Chapter 4

White, *Law in American History*, 245–90, provides more detail on the relationships between law and entrepreneurial activity in the first half of the nineteenth century. See also, in the *Cambridge History*, Bruce H. Mann, "The Transformation of Law and Economy in Early America," 1:365–99; Claire Priest, "Law and Commerce, 1580–1815," 1:400–46; Tony A. Freyer, "Legal Innovation and

Market Capitalism, 1790–1920," 2:449–82; B. Zorina Khan, "Innovations in Law and Technology, 1790–1920," 2:483–530; and John Henry Schlegel, "Law and Economic Change During the Short Twentieth Century," 3:563–612. Khan's book *The Democratization of Invention: Patents and Copyrights in American Economic Development* (Cambridge: Cambridge University Press, 2005) has more detail on the importance of patent law in the late nineteenth century. Herbert Hovenkamp, *Enterprise and American Law, 1836–1937* (Cambridge, Mass.: Harvard University Press, 1991) is the best overview of law and entrepreneurial developments for that period.

Chapter 5

Three articles in the *Cambridge History* provide a good background on the evolution of criminal law and theories of rehabilitation and punishment from the seventeenth through the twentieth centuries. See Michael Meranze, "Penalty and the Colonial Project: Crime, Punishment, and the Regulation of Morals in Early America," 1:178–210; Elizabeth Dale, "Criminal Justice in the United States, 1790–1920: A Government of Laws or Men?" 2:133–67; and Michael Willrich, "Criminal Justice in the United States," 3:195–231. For additional overviews, see Lawrence M. Friedman, *Law in America: A Short History* (New York: Random House, 2002), 73–122, and Hall and Karsten, *Magic Mirror*, 187–207.

Chapter 6

More detail on the themes of this chapter can be found in the *Cambridge History*: Holly Brewer, "The Transformation of Domestic Law," 1:288–323; Normal Basch, "Marriage and Domestic Relations," 2:245–79; and Margot Canady, "Heterosexuality as a Legal Regime," 3:442–71. Michael Grossberg, *Governing the Hearth: Law and the Family in Nineteenth-Century America* (Chapel Hill: University of North Carolina Press, 1985), and Hendrik Hartog, *Man and Wife in America: A History* (Cambridge, Mass.: Harvard University Press, 2000), are useful overviews of the changing state of domestic relations in nineteenth-century America. For twentieth-century developments, see Lawrence M. Friedman, *Private Lives* (Cambridge, Mass.: Harvard University Press, 2004).

Chapter 7

G. Edward White, *Tort Law in America: An Intellectual History*, 2nd ed. (New York: Oxford University Press, 2003), covers many of the themes of this chapter in more detail. John Fabian Witt, *The Accidental Republic* (Cambridge, Mass.: Harvard University Press, 2004), emphasizes the attitudinal shift toward compensation for civil injury that helped fuel both the growth of tort law and the emergence of workers' compensation in that late nineteenth and early twentieth centuries. Kenneth S. Abraham, *The Liability Century* (Cambridge, Mass.: Harvard University Press, 2008), describes the growing interaction between tort law and liability insurance in the twentieth century. The history of tort law is one of the few areas not given coverage in the *Cambridge History*.

Chapter 8

Three essays in the *Cambridge History* provide additional detail on the topics in this chapter: Hugh C. MacGill and R. Kent Newmyer, "Legal Education and Legal Thought, 1799–1920," 2:36–61; William W. Fisher III, "Legal Theory and Legal Education 1920–2000," 3:34–72; and Robert W. Gordon, "The American Legal Profession, 1870–2000," 3:72–126. Robert Stevens, *Law School: Legal Education in America* (Chapel Hill: University of North Carolina Press, 1983), remains the best overview of the history of American law schools. Maxwell Bloomfield, *American Lawyers in a Changing Society* (Cambridge, Mass.: Harvard University Press, 1976), covers the education and professional activities of late eighteenth- and nineteenth-century lawyers, and William P. LaPiana, *Logic and Experience: The Origin of Modern American Legal Education* (New York: Oxford University Press, 1994), discusses the changes in American legal education initiated by Harvard after the Civil War. Craig Evan Klafter, "The Influence of Vocational Law Schools on the Origins of American Legal Thought, 1779–1829," *American Journal of Legal History* 37 (1993): 307–31, underscores the importance of proprietary law schools in late eighteenth- and early nineteenth-century American legal education.

Index

Page numbers in italics refer to illustrations.

A

AALS. *See* Association of American Law Schools
ABA. *See* American Bar Association
abolishment, 22, 23, 25, 27
abolition/abolitionists, 24, 28, 30, 31
abortion, 91, 128
Academy of Motion Pictures, 64
accidents
    compensation scheme for, 109
    in workplace, 105
act of peril liability, 99, 101, 108
Adams, John, 114
admission
    to bar, 115, 117, 118, 119
    to law schools, 118–19, 120–21, 122, 123
adoption, 89
advertising agencies, 59
African Americans
    "pass papers" for, 74
    prison population of, 79
African American slavery, 1
    abolishment of, 22, 23, 25, 27
    abundant agricultural resources due to, 17

American politics and, 25
colonial heritage of, 18–22
commercial prosperity due to, 17
Constitution and, 22–25
in eighteenth century, 18
labor force and, 17
landholding impacted by, 33
law and, 17–31, 127–28
plantations with, 20–21
population growth due to, 17, 20, 27
reexamination of, 21
regional conflict (1800–1860) and, 25–31
significance of, 17
slave codes with, 19
slave courts with, 19
slave patrols, 20, 22
western expansion of, 25–28
agricultural resources, 17
agriculture regulations, 40
allotment program for Indian tribes, 13–14, 15
amendments. *See specific amendments*
America
    cotton and, 26, 27
    "creole elites" in, 34, 113

America (*continued*)
extended household in, 82–84
labor force of, 26–27
land, labor, government, in, 32–35
law in history of, 1–2, 17–31
population growth of, 27
property rights and regulations in history of, 42–44
regional economies of, 28
slavery and politics of, 25
territorial expansion of, 25–26, 28
American Bar Association (ABA), 120–21, 122, 130
American features, of criminal law, 71–72
American Revolution, 115
American Telephone and Telegraph Company, 57
Amerindian tribes, 7, 8, 10, 46. *See also* Indians
Anglo-American heritage, of torts, 96–97, 98
Anglo-American law, 89
antebellum period
eminent domain relating to, 35
property rights and regulations during, 35–36
apprentices, 114–15, 116–17
Articles of Confederation, 115
Association of American Law Schools (AALS), 121, 122, 130
attendance, at law schools, 117
attorneys, 113

B

bar
admission to, 115, 117, 118, 119
associations for, 116, 117
examination, 119, 123
barristers, 112–13, 118
Bill of Rights amendments, 70–71, 78

birth control, 91, 93
Blackstone, William, 82–83, 115
bondsmen, 18
boundary tracing, in police power cases, 36, 38, 39, 43
Bowers v. Hardwick, 94, 95
British colonies, legal education and profession in, 112–16
British Crown, land acquisition and, 46–47
Brown v. Kendall, 98
Brown v. Plata, 80
Bureau of Indian Affairs, 12, 15
Bureau of Internal Revenue, 77
Bureau of Investigation (FBI), 76, 94

C

cable television, 64, 65, 66, 128
capital crime proliferation, 69–70
Cardozo, Benjamin, 104
Cayuga Nation, 15
Charles River Bridge v. Warren Bridge, 53
Cherokee Nation v. Georgia
federal government role in, 10–11
legitimacy issues of, 9
child custody, 87–88, 89
Child Online Protection Act, 66
children, in household, 83, 84–85, 87–88
Christianity, 5
citizenship, property rights with, 43
civil action, 98, 99
civil disobedience, 130
civil injuries, law of torts and
Anglo-American heritage, 96–97
liability insurance (1950–2000), 104–11
negligence principle and tort law expansion (1880–1950), 99–104, 128
torts as common law field, 97–99
civil liability, 98, 101

civil suits, 97
Civil War, 1, 13
  legal profession before and after,
    112, 116, 117, 118, 119, 123
  police forces and, 74, 75, 90
  property rights and, 36, 38
  railroads and, 55, 56
  slavery and, 17, *21*
collective responsibility, for crimes,
  69
College of William and Mary, 114
colonial and revolutionary years,
  legal education and profession
    in, 112–16
colonial and revolutionary years:
  land acquisition
  British Crown involved in, 46–47
  English common law with, 47–48
  freeholder class in, 47
  as investment, 47
  "proprietors," 46
  from tribes, 46
  undeveloped land, 47
colonial courts, 7
colonial heritage, of African
  American slavery, 18–22
colonial years through Constitution
  framing, criminal law during
  amendments relating to, 70–71
  American features of, 71–72
  European settlement punishment,
    69–70
  at state level, 71–72
  tribal punishment, 69–70
Columbia College, 117
Commentaries on American Law
  (Kent), 85, 100, 117
*Commentaries on the Law of
  England* (Blackstone), 82, 115
common law field, tort law as,
  97–99
common law marriages, 86, 87,
  89, 92
common law tort system
  modifications

accident compensation scheme,
  109
compensation system, 107–8
liability insurance and, 104–11
medical malpractice cases, 107
no-fault insurance, 105, 107, 110
statutory workers' compensation,
  104–5, 106
strict liability, 105, 108, 109, 110
third-party liability, 106
The Common Law (Holmes), 99,
  101
Communications Decency Act, 66
communications media emergence
  advertising agencies, 59
  Internet, 66
  legal framework for, *62*, 66, 67
  movies, 64–65, 66–67
  newspapers, 59
  radio, 60–61, *62*
  Supreme Court and, 64–65, 66
  television, 61, 63, 64, 65
compensation system, 107–8
  accident, 109
  for workers, 104–5, 106
Congress, 51, 55, 56, 130
Constitution
  African American slavery and,
    22–25
  framers of, 22, 23, 25, 69–72, 114,
    115, 116
  Full Faith and Credit Clause of,
    24, 29
  government and, 127
  provisions of, 23–24
  Thirteenth Amendment to, 31
constitutionalism, 79, 81
constitutional law, 81
constitutional procedural
  protections, 68, 72, 78
constitutional safeguards, 78, 129
contemporary jurisprudence, of
  property, 41–42
continental boundaries, 49
Continental Congress, 114, 115

contracts, 57–58
copyright protection, 41–42, 58, 128
cotton, 26, 27
courts. *See also* Supreme Court
    colonial, 7
    Marshall Court, 10–11
    slave, 19
"creole elites," in America, 34, 113
crimes
    collective responsibility for, 69
    organized, 78
    proliferation of capital, 69–70
    wars on, 79
criminal act definitions, 68
criminal law, 129
    American features of, 71–72
    colonial years through
        Constitution framing, 69–72
    constitutional procedural
        protections, 68
    criminal act definitions, 68
    federal government's growth
        in, 76
    nineteenth century policing,
        punishment, and, 72–75
    state level of, 71–72
    in twentieth century, 76–81, 129
criminal penalties, in European
    settlements, 69
criminal punishment theories,
    71, 73
cultivation, of land, 33

D

Declaration of Independence, 22,
    114, 115, 116
defective products, 108–9, 110,
    128–29
Defense of Marriage Act, 95
Democracy in America
    (de Tocqueville), 3
Department of Commerce, 60
digital technology, 41, 42
divorce, 86, 87, 89, 90, 91, 92, 128

domestic activity definitions, 90–92
domestic household emergence,
    84–90
domestic partnerships, 94
domestic relations, law and, 82–95,
    128
domestic sphere, 82, 95
    of householding, 84, 88, 91
    of life, 85, 87, 90
    of nuclear families, 89
Dred Scott v. Sandford, 29, 30, 128
dueling, 75

E

economies. *See also* Reconstruction,
    and property, in late
    nineteenth-century economy
    industrialized, 36
    regional, 28
Edison General Electric Company,
    57
Eighteenth Amendment, 77
eighteenth century, slavery in, 18
Eighth Amendment, 71
Eisenstadt v. Baird, 93
Eliot, Charles, 119
eminent domain, 35
English common law, 47–48
English legal profession
    attorneys, 113
    barristers, 112–13, 118
    solicitors, 113, 118
English settlements, 32–33
entrepreneurship, 45–67
environmental practices, of Indian
    tribes, 4
Erie Canal, 53
European immigration, 51–52, 72, 75
European settlements
    accommodations of, 3–4
    capital crime proliferation in,
        69–70
    Christianity in, 5
    colonial courts established by, 7

English, 32–33
hierarchal punishment practices
    of, 70
individual criminal penalties of, 69
public punishments in, 69
war involvement of, 8–9
extended household, in early
    America, 82–84

F

FBI. *See* Bureau of Investigation
Federal Communications
    Commission (FCC), 60, 61, 63,
    64, 65
federal government
    criminal law growth of, 76
    Indians as wards of, 10
    industry and agriculture
        regulated by, 40
    legal role of, 10–11
    tribal land taken by, 14, 15–16, 127
federal legislation, 38, 39
Federal Radio Commission (FRC),
    60–61
Fifth Amendment, 30, 41, 71, 79
First Amendment, 64, 65
Fourteenth Amendment, 36–38,
    64, 79, 90
Fourth Amendment, 71, 78
framers, of Constitution, 22, 23, 25,
    69–72, 114, 115, 116
franchises, 53, 54, 128
FRC. *See* Federal Radio
    Commission
Freedman's Bureau, 90
freeholder class, 47
Fugitive Slave Act, 28
Full Faith and Credit Clause, of
    Constitution, 24, 29

G

General Allotment Act, 13–14
Google, 42

government. *See also* federal
    government
    Constitution and, 127
    labor, land, and, 32–35
grades, in law schools, 122, 123
Greenleaf, Simon, 99
Griswold v. Connecticut, 93

H

Hamilton, Alexander, 114
Harvard Law School, 117, 118–19,
    120
hierarchical punishment practices,
    70
hierarchical ranking, among Indian
    tribes, 4
Holmes, Oliver Wendell, Jr., 99,
    100–101, 118
homosexuality, 94
household
    children in, 83, 84–85, 87–88
    domestic, 84–90
    extended, 82–84
    individuals in, 92–93
    male head of, 84
    master-servant relationship in,
        83, 84, 87
    in twentieth century, 92–95
    women in, 83, 84–85
    workers in, 83–84
householding, domestic sphere of,
    84, 88, 91

I

illegitimacy, 88, 128
immigration
    European, 51–52, 72, 75
    growth of, 72, 75
Indian Reorganization Act, 15
Indians
    collective responsibility for
        crimes, 69
    as federal government wards, 10

Indians (*continued*)
    land titles of, 9, 10
    marginalization of, 1
    as red race, 8, 9
    relocation policies for, 11–12
    "removal" of, 12
    reservations for, 12–13
    as savages, 5, 10
Indian tribes, contact phase with
    conflicts during, 6
    diseases during, 6
    duties during, 5
    environmental practices during, 4
    hierarchical ranking during, 4
    jurisdiction issue during, 6, 7
    legal relationships forged in, 7, 8
    liability issue during, 7
    social interactions during, 5, 7
    territorial disputes during, 6
Indian tribes, legal history of, 7, 8
    Asian ancestors of, 4
    with European settlers, 3–4
    recent history, 15–16
Indian tribes, post-contact phases
        with
    initial stage (1754–1783), 8–9
    second stage (1783–1860), 9–11
    third stage (1860s to 1940s),
        11–14
individuals, in household, 92–93
industrial enterprise (1860–1900),
        law and
    contracts with, 57–58
    copyrights, 58
    land settlement as, 55
    patents, 58–59, 128
    transportation as, 55–57
industrialized economy, 36
industry
    and agriculture regulations, 40
    transcontinental railroads'
        impact on, 56–57
injuries. *See also* civil injuries, law
        of torts and
    intentional, 100
Inns of Court, 113, 118, 130

insurance
    liability, 104–11
    no-fault, 105, 107, 110
intentional injury, 100
Internet, 42, 66
interstate commerce, 36–38
Interstate Commerce Act, 36

J

Jay, John, 114
Jefferson, Thomas, 22, 114
Jeffries, John Calvin, Jr., *124*
Johnson v. McIntosh, 9, 10, 14, 51
judges, 125–26
judiciary, 125
jurisdiction issues, 6, 7
jurisprudence. *See* property rights
        and regulations

K

Kent, James, 85, 100, 117
"King Philip's war, 7
Kings College, 114

L

labor, land, government, and,
        32–35
labor force
    of America, 26–27
    slavery and, 17
labor unions, 73
Lakota tribe, *6*
land. *See also* colonial and
        revolutionary years: land
        acquisition; public lands,
        western migration, and
        transportation sector
        (1800–1860)
    acquisition of, 46–49
    cultivation of, 33
    federal government and tribal,
        14, 15–16
    grants of, 50–51

Indian title to, 9, 10
labor, government, and,
    32–35
ownership of, 32–34
settlement of, 55
undeveloped, 32, 47
landholding, slavery's influence
    on, 33
Langdell, C. C., 119
law. *See also* common law
    marriages; common law tort
    system modifications; criminal
    law; tort law
  Anglo-American, 89
  constitutional, 81
  English common, 47–48
  "rule of law," 2
law, domestic relations and, 128
  domestic activity definitions,
    90–92
  domestic household emergence,
    84–90
  extended household in early
    America, 82–84
  household membership, in
    twentieth century, 92–95
law, entrepreneurship and
  colonial and revolutionary years:
    land acquisition, 46–48
  communications media
    emergence, 59–67
  definition of, 45
  industrial enterprise (1860–1900),
    55–59
  public lands, western migration,
    and transportation sector
    (1800–1860), 48–55
law, in American history
  American Indian tribes
    marginalized by, 1
  Civil War relating to, 1
  issues of, 1–2
  private themes of, 1
  slavery and, 17–31, 127–28
law firms, 123–26
Lawrence v. Texas, 95

law schools, 130
  admission to, 118–19, 120–21,
    122, 123
  attendance at, 117
  cost of, 125
  grades in, 122, 123
  Harvard Law School, 117, 118–19,
    120
  hierarchy of, 122
  Litchfield School of Law, 114
  requirements for, 121, 123
law writs, 97, 98
legal doctrines and policies, 127
legal documents, 127
legal education and profession
  apprentices, 114–15, 116–17
  bar admission, 115, 117, 118, 119
  in British colonies, 112–16
  before and after Civil War, 112,
    116, 117, 118, 119, 123
  colonial and revolutionary years,
    112–16
  judiciary in, 125
  in nineteenth century, 116–21
  proprietary schools, 114, 117,
    119, 122
  status of, 130
  in twentieth century, 121–26
legal framework, for
    communications media, 62,
    66, 67
legal profession. *See* legal education
    and profession
legal relationships, with Indian
    tribes, 7, 8
legal role, of federal government,
    10–11
liability
  act of peril, 99, 101, 108
  civil, 98, 101
  common law tort system and
    insurance for, 104–11
  reduced, 103
  standards of, 98–99
  strict, 105, 108, 109, 110
  third-party, 106

Lincoln, Abraham, *120*
Litchfield School of Law, 114
Lone Wolf v. Hitchcock, 14
Long Island Railroad wreck, *103*
Louisiana Purchase, 9, 26, 48, 52
Loving v. Virginia, 93
lynching, 75

M

MacPherson v. Buick Motor Co.,
    104
Madison, James, 8, 9, 114
male head, of household, 84
marginalization, of Indians, 1
marriages, 90, 128
    common law, 86, 87, 89, 92
    licenses for, *93*
    polygamous, 91
Marshall Court, 10–11
master-servant relationship, 83,
    84, 87
medical malpractice cases, 107
Microsoft, 42
Mississippi River, 52
modern negligence cases, 100, 101,
    102, 104, 111
Monroe, James, 8, 9
movies, 64–65, 66–67
municipal police forces, 74–75

N

natural rights ideology, 22
negligence principle, tort law
    expansion and, 99–104, 128
newspapers, 59
nineteenth century
    criminal law, policing, and
        punishment in, 72–75
    immigrant growth during, 72,
        75
    legal education and profession
        in, 116–21
    penitentiaries during, 73

population growth during, 72, 116
reconstruction and property in
    late, 36–38
rehabilitation emphasized
    during, 73
no-fault insurance, 105, 107, 110
North American secession, 1
Northwest Territory, 51
nuclear families, domestic sphere
    of, 89

O

Oregon Territory, 48
organized crime, 78
ownership, of land, 32–34

P

"pass papers," for African
    Americans, 74
patents, 58–59, 128
penitentiaries, 73
plantations, 20–21
police/policing, 38, 72–75, 90
politics, slavery and, 25
polygamous marriages, 91
population growth
    of America, 27
    during nineteenth century, 72,
        116
    of prison population, 79–80,
        81
    slavery's impact on, 17, 20, 27
primogeniture, 48
prison population increase, 79–80,
    81
prohibition movement, 77
property, profitability of, 43–44
property rights and regulations
    in American history, 42–44
    in antebellum period, 35–36
    boundary tracing and, 36, 38,
        39, 43
    and citizenship, 43

contemporary jurisprudence of,
41–42
federal legislation for, 38, 39
as foundational legal issues, 32
land, labor, government, in early
America, 32–35
for land ownership, 32–34
police power exception to, 38
public welfare and, 43
Reconstruction, late nineteenth-
century economy and, 36–38
state legislation for, 38
Supreme Court and, 36, 39, 40,
41–42, 43
transformation of property rights
jurisprudence (1900–1940),
38–41
for undeveloped land, 32
proprietary schools, 114, 117, 119,
122
proprietors, of colony, 46
public lands, western migration,
and transportation sector
(1800–1860)
Congress's role in, 51
continental boundaries, 49
entrepreneurial venture of, 49
European immigration and,
51–52, 72, 75
franchises and, 53, 54, 128
land acquisition relating to,
48–49
law's role in, 48–55
Mississippi River, 52
public welfare, 43
punishment
constitutional protections
relating to, 72
in European settlements,
69–70
labor unions and, 73
municipal police forces and,
74–75
nineteenth-century policing,
criminal law, and, 72–75

theories of, 71, 73
tribal, 69–70

R

radio
content of, 60–61
networks of, 61
regulation of, 61, *62*
spectrum interference of, 60
railroads. *See* transcontinental
railroads
Reconstruction, and property,
in late nineteenth-century
economy
Fourteenth Amendment relating
to, 36–38
industrialized economy and,
36
interstate commerce and,
36–38
red race, Indians as, 8, 9
Reeve, Tapping, 83
regional conflict (1800–1860),
slavery and, 25–31
regional economies, 28
regulations. *See also* property rights
and regulations
of radio, 61, *62*
rehabilitation, 73, 76
relocation policies, for Indians,
11–12
"removal," of Indians, 12
Republic of California, 48
Republic of Texas, 48
requirements, for law schools, 121,
123
reservations, for Indians, 12–13
Restatement Third, 110
Revolutionary War, 21, 23, 51
revolutionary years. *See* colonial
and revolutionary years, legal
education and profession in;
colonial and revolutionary
years: land acquisition

Roe v. Wade, 93
"rule of law," 2

S

same-sex relationships, 1, *93*, 94, 95, 128
schools. *See also* law schools
  proprietary, 114, 117, 119, 122
Scott, Dred, 29–30
Sedition and Espionage Acts, 76
Shaw, Lemuel, 98
sheriff's sale of house and barn, *37*
Sherman Anti-Trust Act, 36
Sixth Amendment, 71, 79
slavery. *See* African American slavery
slaves
  auction of, *21*
  codes for, 19
  courts for, 19
  patrols for, 20, 22, 72, 74
social interactions, with Indian tribes, 5, 7
solicitors, 113, 118
spectrum interference, 60
state legislation, 38
state level, of criminal law, 71–72
Story, Joseph, 117
strict liability, 105, 108, 109, 110
subversive activity, 76
Supreme Court, 1
  cases heard by, 9, 10, 14, 29, 30, 53, 58, 93, 94, 129
  communications media and, 64–65, 66
  constitutional law requirement by, 81
  polygamy and, 91
  property rights and, 36, 39, 40, 41–42, 43
  published reports from, 118
  trade secrets ruling by, 41
Swift v. Tyson, 58

T

television
  cable, 64, 65, 66, 128
  FCC and, 61, 63, 64, 65
  First Amendment challenge to, 64, 65
  UHF, 63, 64
  VHF, 63, 64
territorial disputes, with Indian tribes, 6
territorial expansion, 25–26, 28
third-party liability, 106
Thirteenth Amendment, 31, 90
de Tocqueville, Alexis, 3–4
tort law. *See also* civil injuries, law of torts and
  as common law field, 97–99
  conduct relating to, 102
  definition of, 96–97
  doctrines of, 102–3, 104, 129
  intentional injury, 100
  modern negligence cases, 100, 101, 102, 104, 111
  negligence principle and expansion of, 99–104, 128
  Restatement Third of, 110
torts. *See also* common law tort system modifications
  Anglo-American heritage of, 96–97, 98
trade secrets, 41
transcontinental railroads
  funds for, 55–56
  growth of, 56
  industry impacted by, 56–57
transformation of property rights jurisprudence (1900–1910), 38–41
transportation. *See also* public lands, western migration, and transportation sector (1800–1860)
  and industrial enterprise, 55–57

tribal land, federal government and, 14, 15–16, 127
tribal punishment, 69–70
tribes. *See also* Indian tribes, contact phase with; Indian tribes, legal history of; Indian tribes, post-contact phases with
  Amerindian, 7, 8, 10, 46
  Lakota, 6
  land acquisition from, 46
twentieth century
  household membership in, 92–95
  legal education in, 121–23
  legal profession in, 123–26
twentieth-century criminal law
  constitutionalism, 79, 81
  constitutional safeguards, 78, 129
  federal government growth in, 76
  organized crime, 78
  prohibition movement, 77
  subversive activity, 76

U

ultra high frequency (UHF) television channels, 63, 64
undeveloped land, 32, 47

V

very high frequency (VHF) television channels, 63, 64
vigilante justice, 75
Volstead Act, 77

W

wagon train, 50
war involvement, of European settlements, 8–9
Warren, Earl, 78
wars, on crime, 79
Washington, George, 114
western boundary line, 8, 9
western expansion, of slavery, 25–28
western migration. *See* public lands, western migration, and transportation sector (1800–1860)
Westinghouse Electric Company, 57
women, in household, 83, 84–85
Worcester v. Georgia, 10, 11
workers, in household, 83–84
workers' compensation, 104–5, 106
workplace accidents, 105
World Trade Center, 125